A Guide for New Public Speaking Teachers
Building Toward Success

Third Edition

Calvin L. Troup
Duquesne University

PEARSON

Boston   New York   San Francisco
Mexico City   Montreal   Toronto   London   Madrid   Munich   Paris
Hong Kong   Singapore   Tokyo   Cape Town   Sydney

ISBN 0-205-43893-8

Printed in the United States of America

10 9 8 7 6 5 4 3 2 1   09 08 07 06 05 04

Contents

Chapter Three: Putting the Plan into Action   56

Introduction

Teaching public speaking is not rocket science. Rocket science is simpler. It relies on fixed formulas and predictable physical laws and conditions. By contrast, as a public speaking instructor you will deal with human beings learning an ancient art form through which the course of history has been fashioned and refashioned. People have been teaching others to speak in public contexts for 5,000 years or more. Therefore, as you prepare to teach, you join an ancient tradition in the academy. You may find yourself teaching public speaking with or without broad speaking experience yourself, with or without teaching experience in a college classroom, and with or without a deep theoretical foundation in the field of Communication. You may teach the course in any of a number of various instructional circumstances. But whatever the teaching circumstance, your approach to the classroom, your understanding of the special challenges presented by public speaking, and your knowledge of available support will be crucial to your effectiveness.

As you begin, remember that students are resilient. Speakers, even inexperienced ones, are inclined to make significant progress if given the opportunity, including a favorable learning environment, good reasons and good reasoning to accompany their practice of the art, and high expectations from their instructor. Also remember that you must seek to embody excellence as a speaker, as an aid to students as learners and practitioners. Finally, never forget that you are preparing to teach a basic public speaking course. I was privileged to hear Carroll Arnold, a distinguished Communication scholar and major contributor to the development of the discipline, share his wisdom with new public speaking instructors in the twilight of his life. His most memorable remarks called for simplicity. He explained that each semester he spent teaching the course, he aimed at only three learning objectives for students: to organize their messages; to adapt their messages to the audience; to speak extemporaneously. Your objectives may vary, but basics will lead to effectiveness. Students can make significant progress in their public speaking knowledge and ability when you stick to the basics.

Approach to the Classroom: Teaching as a Scholar

You have choices about your orientation toward the classroom. On one hand, you may regard teaching undergraduates as an evil necessary to achieving your scholarly goals. On the other hand, you may regard yourself as an educator who works in different modes but always with the same basic calling, whether in the classroom, library, or study. Practically speaking, Communication scholars rarely pursue their research to the exclusion of teaching. Some professors consider teaching introductory courses a waste of time and an unwelcome diversion from their scholarship. However, the best seek out connections between their scholarship and how they teach every course, including the basic public speaking course. Whether you choose to see teaching and scholarship as mutually exclusive activities or as connected and integrated modes of the same vocation, your choice will be reflected in your attitude and performance as a public speaking teacher. This manual proceeds from the standpoint and expectation that you should be constantly exploring relevant connections between your own learning and the courses you teach. Make the classroom a site where you can incorporate what you are learning, explore and test emerging thought, and generate new questions through the readings, activities, and assignments you select for the course. As you begin to accomplish the integration of your teaching and scholarship, the quality of each should improve, as should the learning experience of your students.

The Special Challenges of the Public Speaking Course

Reflect on the basic public speaking class as it was taught at the college or university where you did your bachelor's degree; think over the variety of challenges presented by the course. As an instructor, you will need to take stock of these challenges and prepare yourself to address them.

Required Course

On many campuses public speaking is a requirement. Therefore, so many students take the public speaking course that their expectations, informed by the student culture, may rival the expectations set by the department and instructor. The course's degree of difficulty and techniques for getting a good grade in it are part of the campus lore. Most commonly, students expect to get a good grade in public speaking with a minimal amount of effort. Students know they are taking an introduction to public speaking, a course not ordinarily used to screen out students from competitive majors or programs. Many students in the course are not Communication majors. They may have a mistaken tendency to view Communication as a less serious field of study than their own. Not every student will know these factors on the first day of class, but many will find out what to expect from public speaking from talking to friends and acquaintances early in the term.

Underprepared Students

Most students come into public speaking woefully under-prepared. Education has made them well acquainted with the written word, but the same education has neglected the spoken word. Education critics attack secondary schools that fail to teach all of their students to read and write, but no such standard exists for public speaking. Functionally, most adults think eloquence is a gift, not a skill; secondary school curricula reflect this opinion. From kindergarten on, formal education is primarily an exercise in literacy training: learning to read, write, and figure. Less than half of your students are likely to have had a high school course in public speaking. Many will have experienced token oral assignments in English class or some other subject, but will not have any theoretical understanding of the speaking situation or systematic skill training. Some will have public speaking experience outside of the classroom. But take a moment to compare how long they have been writing and reading sentences, paragraphs, essays, and books with the time spent on understanding and performance of public, spoken language. In sum, you will be teaching college-level literate minds, most of whom have sub-collegiate understanding and skill in the art of public speaking.

New Cognitive Skills

You will introduce students to oral patterns of thought and language for public contexts, arts quite foreign to many literate people. Their initial inclination would be to write out a speech as if it were an essay, and then read it to the class or memorize it for delivery. When you ask students to speak extemporaneously, you are asking them to awaken latent cognitive skills and develop patterns of thought that they may admire in other speakers but believe to be personally unattainable. They possess some of the necessary capability in conversational speech, yet the transition from conversation to public speaking is not a one-to-one transfer. Literacy skills may assist in learning about public speaking and in researching speeches. But the design and performance of their presentations must be grounded in preparing and producing the spoken word without memorization, and in understanding how listeners receive the spoken word versus the written word.

Danger: Teaching Skill without Theory

As a result, instructors may be tempted to offer a simplistic course oriented toward practice alone, devoting most class sessions to speeches and speaking exercises. Even with minimal instruction, many people will improve their speaking skills dramatically by being forced to speak for a grade a number of times in succession. But when the primary objective becomes making inexperienced speakers feel more comfortable in front of groups, we rob students of the knowledge they need to integrate performance and theory, the why behind the how. The aim of any public speaking course should be to equip students with integrated knowledge and skill in the art, so that they can continue to advance as speakers long after completing the course.

In-Class Speaking Time

Even when we strike a good balance between instruction and speaking assignments, speeches must be given in class, which puts instructional time at a premium. In other courses, we assign major course projects to be completed outside of class. However, a well-balanced public speaking course still requires one-third to one-half of the class sessions for student speeches. Therefore, teachers must maximize the use of class sessions dedicated to instruction and utilize the inherent instructional opportunities in every speaking round.

Practicing What You Preach

In public speaking the instructor not only teaches content, but also models speaking performance. You bear a broader instructional burden in public speaking than in most courses, simply because students should scrutinize how you present yourself and the course material. Thankfully, you will not need to perform perfectly, but no public speaking instructor escapes the realization that while we teach public speaking we employ the skills we teach. If you lack speaking experience, concentrate on practicing what you are preaching. If you possess confidence as a speaker, draw attention to learnable skills and strategies as you use them, and try to improve as a speaker every time you enter the classroom.

Evaluating and Grading Speeches

The activity that presents the greatest challenge to students in the course—giving speeches—also presents the greatest challenge for instructors—evaluating and grading their students' performances. Providing good comments and an accurate assessment of performance requires instructors to manage effectively a variety of dynamics in the course and classroom. Of particular note are student concerns about subjectivity in grading, the competing roles you play as coach and judge, the practical process of writing evaluations, and time spent on speech grading. When evaluations are conducted equitably and efficiently, they advance the quality of the course dramatically. Conversely, new instructors often practice grade inflation or deflation, use grades improperly to motivate students, or waste time that should be devoted to other duties on marathon speech grading sessions. Furthermore, improper handling of speech grading, particularly tardiness in grading and returning speech evaluations, may be the most volatile issue of instructional competence in the basic public speaking course.

Textbook and Supporting Materials for the Basic Course

Become intimately familiar with your textbook. A textbook is only as good as your ability to recognize and communicate its value to your students. Obviously, in a college classroom your task is to teach public speaking, not merely to review a textbook. But instructors who use a textbook wisely may better help their students overcome the lack of preparation, need for theoretical knowledge, and limited in-class instruction time mentioned previously. A good textbook serves as a touchstone for students throughout their public speaking experience.

In public speaking, you can weave the textbook into your course to cultivate student learning, without ever giving a "read your book!" speech in class. The role of the text in your class and how to use it most effectively will be discussed in detail in Chapter Three. For now, recognize that a good public speaking text can save you substantial amounts of preparation time and enhance the learning process for students inside and outside of class. Allyn & Bacon provides extensive support to help you get the most out of the text in your course. This training manual, along with supplements for students that may be required or offered as optional materials, is just one example of the broad spectrum of resources available to assist your in-class instruction.

If you are using one of the below public speaking texts, contact your Allyn & Bacon sales representative to learn more about the wide range of supplemental materials at your disposal intended to enhance student learning.

Public Speaking: An Audience-Centered Approach, by Steven A. Beebe and Susan J. Beebe.

The Elements of Public Speaking, by Joseph A. DeVito.

Principles of Public Speaking, by Kathleen German, Bruce E. Gronbeck, Douglas Ehninger, and
    Alan H. Monroe.

Mastering Public Speaking, by George L. Grice and John F. Skinner.

Principles and Types of Public Speaking, by Raymie E. McKerrow, Bruce E. Gronbeck,
    Douglas Ehninger, and Alan H. Monroe.

Public Speaking: Strategies for Success, by David Zarefsky.

Each of these texts has been used successfully nationwide. All six effectively cover the basic principles of public speaking, but do so with distinctive emphases and unique features. Chapter Five of this manual provides a grid of corresponding activities and exercises you can use to teach basic concepts and principles from each of the textbooks. Refer to the grid to find additional ideas or specific emphases available in Allyn & Bacon textbooks other than the one adopted for your course.

The Plan of . . . *Building toward Success*

The basics of public speaking have not changed dramatically over the centuries; nor have the challenges. However, as the emphases of textbooks reflect, approaches to the course vary widely. Each college or university generates a different cultural setting for the course and serves a different community. Whatever the approach on your campus, *Building Toward Success* is designed to assist you in addressing the basic issues and challenges intrinsic to the course, emphasizing how the structure of the course in your context, your preparation, and support from textbooks and other resources can assist you in navigating the basic public speaking course.

I.   Chapter One leads you through an assessment of the **context** for your particular course and choices you must make concerning how to frame your course at this particular moment in the life of your department, institution, and the field of Communication.

II. You complete **pre-term preparations** in Chapter Two, which lead you from considering your multiple roles as an instructor, through how a textbook and other resources can support the course, to the structure and final syllabus to be distributed to students.

III. Chapter Three provides a brief introduction to **teaching methods** and **standard instructional components** from which to build an effective class session. You will find options and strategies for conducting speaking rounds as well as special issues related to the first day of class.

IV. The special challenges of **grading** in the public speaking course, particularly speech grading, are addressed in Chapter Four.

V. In Chapter Five, you will consider some **routine problems** new instructors face and common questions most of us have asked as we teach public speaking the first time, questions such as: "How do I balance my other responsibilities with my teaching?" "I don't have a prior degree in Communication; how can I best handle this assignment?" "How can I maintain a free speech environment regarding religious and ideological positions when I suspect that speakers will seriously offend other class members?"

VI. The **matrix of Allyn & Bacon textbook chapters** appears in Chapter Six, after a list of the texts. The chapter also directs you to additional support materials and public speaking resources available to instructors through Allyn & Bacon.

Chapter One:

Framing the Public Speaking Course

Whether you like it or not, teaching involves you in the life of an institution and perhaps several institutions. The public speaking course you teach is located in time and space. Whole histories, traditions, communities, disciplines, and varieties of culture have contributed to the situation you and your students will work through as a class. You will do well to familiarize yourself with the particular constraints and opportunities of the situation in which you will serve as an instructor. You and your students will contribute in some way to the tradition of the public speaking course at your institution. To contribute well, you must develop a keen sense for your historical moment. That will mean assessing the current mission of the course in the life of your university, department, and discipline; setting definite objectives for your particular section(s); and grasping the rationale behind conventions incorporated in most public speaking courses today.

Deliberation in a Democratic Republic

Public speaking has deep cultural roots in Western culture, particularly in the United States and Canada. The tradition of public speaking instruction is decisively linked to democratically-constituted societies in which democratic forms of government continue to function. Basic principles of democracy include a commitment to deliberation by citizens involved in civic decision-making through electoral politics and influence upon elected representatives, other officials, and government organizations. Traditionally, the communication paradigm for the right and ability to express oneself effectively in democratic society has been public speaking. Despite the proliferation of electronic means of communication, public speaking remains the predominant art associated with deliberation—the core of democratic practice. The social goods associated with deliberation remain a primary impetus for teaching the art of public speaking on college and university campuses today.

The Course in Your Community

Democracy, higher education, and public speaking instruction share deep old roots. Much of the record we have of public speaking in the ancient world—ordinarily called rhetoric— comes from master scholars of antiquity who earned their living by teaching people to advocate and defend their ideas and selves in their own communities. Of course they argued about methods, ethics, effects, and social implications, which constitutes most of what we have in addition to surviving manuals and lecture notes. Most of them taught and wrote on a great deal more than public speaking as well. The point is that instruction in public speaking seems to predate written history in at least some human civilizations. Early historical records appear with public speaking teachers already on the scene and more-or-less gainfully employed—teaching concepts, methods, and skills inseparable from the local, temporal context.

At various times public speaking instruction has taken the form of training in rhetoric, oratory, or elocution. Sometimes it has been referred to as declamation. In certain times and places in the Western world, courses in public speaking all but evaporated. Rhetorical ideas and skills initially associated with oratory shifted almost entirely to the written word. More recently, the advent of quantitative and qualitative social scientific approaches to Communication has further expanded our ideas about public speaking. Although common ideas are woven through the historical tapestry that constitutes the background to your public speaking class, the teaching has varied markedly from moment to moment and place to place; people were not all teaching the same thing and merely applying different labels. Public speaking courses reflect and shape the particular needs of the communities in which they emerge as an essential component of liberal higher education. When taught well, public speaking courses can become indispensable to the life of such communities. You must seek to understand the particular community in which your course is offered and frame it clearly for students in terms of the college or university, department, and discipline.

Institution: Mission, History, and Student Culture

At one public university, a story is told about how the public speaking course became a graduation requirement for all bachelor's degree candidates. A certain engineering professor was working with a superior doctoral student. At the end of his work at the university, the new Ph.D. was interviewed for a top industry position in the field. Part of the interview required a presentation of his research, which flopped. He did not get the position. Some time later, when the professor became president of the university, one of his first official acts was to make the basic public speaking course an undergraduate requirement for every student.

What is the mission of the college or university in which you will teach public speaking? How is the mission connected to the history and tradition of the school? The educational missions and histories of institutions vary widely, even within similar categories. For instance, knowing that you are teaching in a university classified in a certain way provides little information to help you understand the institutional framework of your course. Most colleges and universities today have produced mission statements and written documentation on the history and mission of the institution. Read them carefully. But official documents and a school's reputation merely approximate the experience of students and faculty. As the story about the basic course at one university suggests, many aspects of the course you will be teaching may be tied to unwritten portions of history and particular interpretations of the mission statement. The course director, department chair, and other faculty members should be able to provide you with a fuller sense of institutional history and how the mission is being implemented.

Consciously contextualize the course within the mission, history, and life of the institution in which you serve—when you get to the point of teaching the course, members of the community should recognize its fit. By no means does a proper fit suggest that every instructor's course should be identical to other sections of the course, past or present. To the contrary, you will bring a unique perspective and personal approach to the course. Also, institutional cultures and communities are dynamic places. Simply remember that no public speaking course belongs to you alone. You have primary responsibility for instruction and a well-defined role as the classroom instructor, but avoid the error of proceeding as though the course was yours alone.

If you are attentive to them, your students will instruct you quickly enough about the fact that every public speaking course is a collaborative, community experience. They will bring their own perspectives on the institution, its mission, and campus life. If possible, talk to a number of colleagues to begin to get a sense for student expectations of the public speaking course on your campus. In larger universities, bookstores often carry fall guidebooks for freshmen, which rate the difficulty and common workload for required courses. Although accuracy of such reports varies, you should be familiar with how the course is perceived by the student culture. On smaller campuses, you will probably have to rely on casual conversations with students. Do not be surprised by what you may discover. For instance, public speaking courses have a reputation for being contributors to grade inflation—an "easy *A*." In some cases freshmen dominate the course, which is oriented to introduce them to college-level studies, while in others students put off taking the course until the latest possible term before graduation. The workload expected in the course varies widely as do the actual number of speeches. You may choose to accentuate the positive attributes and ameliorate the negatives, but you need a sense for what students expect when they walk into your classroom.

The importance of recognizing the interdependence of the public speaking course with the institution at large can be seen through an example of what can happen when we neglect such a perspective. A liberal arts college with some strong professional programs once required all students to take a public speaking course. A member of the faculty from another department in the college explained that the course was so weak and the instruction was so poor that the faculty decided to eliminate the course entirely and added public speaking requirements across the rest of the curriculum instead. In other words, public speaking teachers lost a sense for the importance and connection of the course to the college and provided substandard instruction. Students now receive no grounding in the art of public speaking; they merely receive occasional opportunities to practice without learning the substance of the art of public speaking.

There were certainly other factors—academic and political—that contributed to the demise of the public speaking course at the institution. But the example is not isolated; many courses suffer such fates when they lose connection to the life of the larger institution. Therefore, make it your business to build a comprehensive profile of the school from a variety of perspectives and get a head start on how various constituencies perceive the public speaking course.

Department: Linking the Institution and the Discipline

Most frequently, public speaking courses are offered through the Communication or Speech Communication department. The department—your home as a teacher and a scholar—mediates between the institution, with which you should now be somewhat familiar, and the scholarly discipline of Communication. Give students a sense of how the course and your department fit within both realms. The department bridges two important intellectual communities of which you are a de facto member: the institutional community and the community of Communication scholars. You live and work in both of them, a fact that should become evident to your students. Your classroom may be the first exposure that students have to someone working in the field of Communication as a scholar and practitioner. The course will not only influence their perceptions of what it takes to speak effectively in public, but will also give them a distinct impression about what sort of questions interest people who study Communication and how they address such questions. The quality of your instruction and the dynamism of your classroom as a learning environment should connect you to the discipline and your work as a Communication scholar. Expect interesting questions about Communication to emerge from within your institutional community, particularly through interaction with your students in the learning process.

Discipline: Yesterday, Today, and Tomorrow

You have a unique opportunity to introduce your students to the field of Communication through the public speaking course. On some occasions, instructors attempt to use the public speaking course as a promotional opportunity for the discipline by devoting a class session or two to talking about the Communication field. We should recognize our promotional opportunities, but public speaking class does not lend itself well to surveying the possibilities for students within the field. Neither does the course seem well suited to become a forum in which entire class sessions are dedicated to recruiting majors or minors for the department. However, as we have noted earlier, public speaking does play a foundational role in the history of the discipline, present thought and practice, and considerations for the future of Communication.

Students should leave the course with a well-developed awareness of the role of public speaking in their society and with some sense of how they can use their skills and knowledge to contribute to their communities today and tomorrow. Help them to get situated historically, understanding how and why the course is being taught from both an institutional and disciplinary perspective. For example, students will be glad to hear occasionally about exercises and assignments from history through which they no longer are forced to suffer. They will also appreciate your clear explanations for the conceptual and skill demands currently being placed upon them—especially the connections you can make for them to their anticipated worlds beyond college. If you can make these connections, students will begin to grasp the pertinence of Communication study to the world today and to the future.

Through the term, weave into the course your most interesting communication questions that have clear connections to various aspects of public speaking. For example:

- How does a speaker call a particular audience into existence?

- What do we know about what a speaker can do to help the audience listen well?

- To what degree does the audience participate in the creation of the message?

When you raise theoretical issues close to your own interests, you will naturally demonstrate genuine enthusiasm for the discipline. Looking for such connections should energize your classroom manner as well, giving students a much better sense for the intellectual substance, demands, and attractiveness of the Communication field than a rehearsal of hypothetical applications or job prospects.

Mission and Objectives of Your Course

How would you answer a student who asked, "Why should I take your public speaking course?" You should have a succinct response and rationale in your own mind that any student could understand. The answer should concentrate first on the basic concepts and skills you want each student to master within the framework of your institution, department, and the discipline. Although you should present the mission and objectives of the course to a student in the order listed above, the development should probably begin with the department and move to concepts and skills.

Connection to Departmental Mission

The course you teach should be purposely linked to the mission of your department. As noted earlier, the department integrates the field of Communication and your institutional community. The mission and objectives of the course should be clearly connected to both. Review the recurring emphases and themes in your own department. Whether or not the department has formalized a mission statement, how would you state the departmental mission in your own words? How does the course fit into the mission of the department? Think about questions like these:

- How many students take the course in a given semester or in the school year?

- Are Communication majors required to take public speaking?

- What range of people teaches public speaking for the department?

- What relationship, if any, exists between the course and funding for graduate students?

- Does a faculty member direct the course? If so, how much divergence exists between different sections of the course? If not, what kind of direction comes from the department on teaching the course?

As you begin to fashion your approach to the course, a course calendar, assignments, and policies, make sure that they complement the larger mission of the department.

Specific Course Mission

The official course description is a good place from which to launch your version of the public speaking course. How does the catalog of courses describe public speaking? Notice the similarities and differences in emphasis and specificity in the following course descriptions for public speaking courses. The selections come from institutions that vary widely in size, mission, location, etc. (Course numbers and other school-specific requirements have been omitted. All information comes from Internet sites, which can be accessed on the NCA home page list of Communication Departments.)

- *Public Presentations: Theory and Practice.* Basic elements of the theory and method of effective and responsible public address; practice in a variety of speech situations; relevant technology; analysis and criticism. BRADLEY UNIVERSITY

- *Essentials of Public Speaking.* Composition and delivery of speeches to inform and persuade. Logical organization is stressed. CALIFORNIA STATE UNIVERSITY— LONG BEACH

◆ *Public Speaking.* [Public Speaking] is a course that provides you the opportunity to improve your skills in public speaking. In our global society, finding one's "voice" in issues relevant to local, national, and international issues requires both personal reflection and critical thought. This course is designed to help hone those skills that can help you become a more informed, proficient, and well-spoken member of both academic and business communities. COLORADO STATE UNIVERSITY

◆ *Public Speaking.* Practical and psychological principles of persuasive speech and negotiating. GENEVA COLLEGE

◆ *Public Speaking.* Develops communication skills necessary to analyze verbal discourse and to perform effectively in public speaking situations that confront the educated person. DUQUESNE UNIVERSITY

◆ *Public Communication.* Study and practice of the basic techniques of public speaking used to inform and persuade audiences. Emphasis on the speech-building process: research, composition, organization, style, delivery, and criticism. GEORGE WASHINGTON UNIVERSITY

◆ *Public Presentations.* This course introduces students to the theory and practice of public speaking. Topics covered include methods of organizing a speech and delivery, the types and uses of evidence, and the effective use of visual aids. Students prepare and deliver several speeches including an informative speech, a persuasive speech and occasional speech, and a career simulation. HOPE COLLEGE

◆ *Speaker-Audience Communication.* Study of rhetorical theory and its application to the preparation, presentation, and criticism of oral discourse in audience situations. Special consideration of listening behavior and of the ethical conduct of speech in a free society. This course fulfills the College oral communication requirement. KANSAS UNIVERSITY

- *Public Speaking.* An advanced course in communication principles to develop skills in the analysis and presentation of speeches. MANKATO STATE UNIVERSITY

- *Introduction to Public Speaking.* Preparation, presentation, and criticism of speeches. Emphasis on the development of public speaking techniques through constructive criticism. UNIVERSITY OF MONTANA

- *Public Speaking.* Theory and extensive practice in various types of speaking. UNIVERSITY OF NORTH CAROLINA—CHAPEL HILL

- *Effective Speech.* Introduction to speech communication: formal speaking, group discussion, analysis and evaluation of messages. Principles of communication, implemented through presentation of speeches, with some attention to group discussion and message evaluation. PENN STATE UNIVERSITY

- *Presentational Communication.* This course develops students' ability to research complex issues, organize facts, develop proposals, and competently deliver formal presentations to audiences. Presentational Communication curriculum offers a blend of public speaking skills (analytical, theoretical, and practical) and audience analysis skills (socio-demographic and psychological) to improve the effectiveness of students' oral communication, critical thinking, and listening skills. UNIVERSITY OF PUGET SOUND

- *Public Speaking.* Study of the principles of public address to include the preparation and delivery of various types of speeches. STETSON UNIVERSITY

- *Public Speaking.* Training in speeches of social and technical interest designed to teach students to develop and illustrate ideas and information and to inform, stimulate, and persuade their audiences. TEXAS A&M UNIVERSITY

Note that while all the courses listed above seem to assume a performance component in the course—that students will actually present speeches in class—the pedagogical objectives for the courses differ. The specific mission of your course should provide more detail than a course catalog description. It should begin to answer the student question "Why take public speaking?" How much emphasis will be placed on preparation, organization, delivery, listening, critical thinking, types of speeches, research, visual support (conventional and electronic), theory, evidence, ethics, psychology, politics, business, academics, group speaking? Your version of the course will not be able to include everything, so the mission should explain the focus and provide some basic reasons for the direction to be taken in the course.

Basic Course Objectives

To answer the question "Why should I take your public speaking course?" decisively, you need to outline objectives that make the mission of the course concrete. What are the principles, concepts, and skills that you expect students to learn? The list you state should be simple—not exhaustive, but three to five main objectives. Nevertheless, make them specific enough that at the end of the term, students could have a good sense for whether the objectives were accomplished. A careful inspection of the textbook might get you started in this process. But most textbooks are designed to support your work in the course—you will still need to be selective about how to use the textbook and other resources. Remember Carroll Arnold's simple set of objectives—at the conclusion of the course, public speaking students should be able to organize their messages, adapt their messages to an audience, and speak extemporaneously. The following examples show three variations on course missions and sets of objectives:

	Mission	Objectives
Course 1	To build competence at preparing and presenting speeches in a variety of workplace and community contexts.	1. To organize a message.
		2. To adapt a message to the audience.
		3. To speak individually and in group contexts.
		4. To speak extemporaneously.
Course 2	To build competence in critical analysis and presentation of spoken public discourse.	1. To conduct critical analysis of public messages.
		2. To research a message.
		3. To organize a message.
		4. To speak extemporaneously.
Course 3	To build presentational competence grounded in theoretical understanding of public speaking situations and practices.	1. To conceptualize the dynamics of speaking situations and practices.
		2. To organize a message.
		3. To adapt a message to the audience.
		4. To speak extemporaneously.

Given the status of your course within the department, institution, and field of Communication, record the mission of your course and a set of course objectives that answer the question "Why take public speaking?"

Extemporaneous Speaking

As you probably noticed, every set of objectives in the preceding table includes "To speak extemporaneously." Each of the six Allyn & Bacon public speaking textbooks mentioned earlier focuses on extemporaneous delivery. Were you to survey every public speaking textbook published in the past 25 years, you would be hard-pressed to find one that encourages students to write a manuscript, to memorize their speech, or to speak impromptu. (Most make exceptions for impromptu speaking under circumstances that precludes adequate preparation.)

Predominance in public speaking courses

Introductory courses in public speaking are dominated by the extemporaneous method of delivery. Although most textbooks explain four delivery alternatives—memorization, manuscript, impromptu, and extemporaneous—a quick review of their pages reveals that the methods taught deal almost exclusively with extemporaneous speaking. As David Zarefsky explains in his public speaking text:

> Extemporaneous presentation . . . is generally recommended for most speakers and speeches, because it encourages a conversational quality and is flexible enough to permit adaptation. Extemporaneous speaking is not impromptu; the speaker has planned the speech carefully, has a specific structure in mind, and probably has outlined the speech and prepared notes for use during presentation. But it also is not memorized or

manuscript; the word-for-word text does not exist in advance of the speaker's delivery. In other words, the speech is prepared and rehearsed, but it is neither written out nor memorized. (354)

Extemporaneous speaking has been practiced from the beginning of recorded history. However, in many historical moments, students were expected to memorize famous speeches or other literature. Experienced public speaking teachers continue to meet students who were taught to memorize or write manuscripts for their presentations in high school Speech or English courses. Nevertheless, we have geared the overwhelming majority of college public speaking courses toward extemporaneous speaking today and that almost exclusively. Why?

Rationale for Emphasis

People in the general public still think about a speech as "written." Indeed, most of the political speeches, news coverage, and commentary seen and heard by the public on media outlets are variations on manuscript speaking. But public speaking pedagogy assumes that such presentations constitute a small fraction of all of the public speaking that goes on in the world on any given day. The depth of commitment to extemporaneous speaking emerges from at least three commonplaces: practical considerations; superior preparation for the whole range of speaking situations; theoretical commitments.

Practice

Most of the presentations people give should be delivered extemporaneously. Through the course of their working lives and beyond, most students will need extemporaneous delivery skills much more than any other presentation method. The majority of workplace speaking situations are best suited to such presentations. But many presenters work without any grasp of extemporaneous delivery, use other methods, and communicate in a mediocre fashion (to which people have grown accustomed). If our students can learn strong extemporaneous speaking skills, then they stand to improve the communication in their workplaces and communities as well as advancing their ideas effectively.

Transferability

Extemporaneous speaking places a wider variety of demands on students, and prepares them to perform the other methods of delivery more effectively, if necessary. Speakers accustomed to developing extemporaneous speeches are more likely to write manuscripts addressed to the ears of the audience—writing for the ear rather than the eye. Likewise, they will be less fearful about eye contact and the broad range of non-verbal communication at their disposal, recognizing the need for fuller communication with the audience, whether speaking from the pages of a manuscript or from memory. Extemporaneous speaking introduces students to the contrast between the spoken and written word and helps them to begin to train themselves in oral practices and performance.

Theory

Extemporaneous speaking rests on a solid conceptual base. Even if there were not such remarkable practical advantages to extemporaneous delivery, most Communication scholars would advocate the method based on theoretical grounds, such as the transactional nature of human communication—the idea that human beings in face-to-face contact are simultaneously sending, interpreting, generating, and receiving messages. Therefore, speakers who can employ a delivery method that promotes full participation with the audience in a transactional mode are positioned to communicate most effectively. Speakers need to read and respond to audience feedback during the presentation. For a prepared message, only extemporaneous delivery allows for such interchanges with the audience.

As mentioned in the Introduction, communication transactions in the public speaking context rely on the spoken word. Therefore, when we speak in public, we should rely on oral patterns of thought and language. Walter Ong presents a valuable theoretical starting point on the unique dynamics of the spoken word in his landmark book, *Orality and Literacy*.

In the book, Ong makes teaching the spoken word an imperative for public speaking courses. Teachers and texts owe our students the extemporaneous emphasis on the word spoken and heard because orality, not literacy, dominates public speaking transactions. Approaching public speaking situations primarily through literate means of cognition and reception compromises the potential quality of the communication for all the parties involved.

Evaluation and Grading

You will be able to do a more satisfying job of evaluating speeches if you can understand the context, mission, and objectives of the course on your campus and embrace the emphasis on extemporaneous speaking. If you view your classroom as a generic public speaking course with generic students and generic standards for evaluation, then you will have a most difficult task. Why? Speech is a distinctive, dynamic human trait, at once most common among us and yet a clear marker of personal identity. Generic criteria are a starting point, but you must put them to work as you have situated and adapted criteria for speaking excellence within the context of the particular course and the specific class that you are evaluating.

Setting Standards

Make the standards for evaluation in your course and in each assignment clear. As you define the mission, objectives, and context of your course, you also begin to frame the concrete standards for evaluation toward which your students will strive. For example, an emphasis on public deliberation enables you to evaluate topic selection for its relevance and evidence for its substance, credibility, and currency in the historical moment. If speaking in organizational contexts is emphasized, then issues tied to conventional expectations for presentations in the workplace, language, appearance, and structure can be evaluated more precisely. Provide clear targets and practices that they can understand by which you can then grade their work.

Establishing Expectations for Grading Performances

Let students know that grading plays an important role for learning in the public speaking course. Not all student anxiety is bad; some stress is productive and necessary. Therefore, introduce students early to the fact that grading will be serious and substantial. Good speech evaluation is crucial to their growth, not a necessary evil, and you need to prepare them for this aspect of the course. They should know clearly that real audiences will be oblivious to how much effort a speaker has put into preparing a speech, and will be brutally realistic in their evaluations in the workplace and public life. Students need to understand that evaluation in a performance environment is different than most traditional academic grading contexts. Also, liberate them from the notion that grading will have any connection to whether their classmates seemed to "like" the speech or even say that they "like" the speech. If you do this well, then they will understand why they got a lower grade than someone whose delivery was less polished than their own, but who followed through on other aspects of the speaking assignment more effectively.

Chapter Two:
Preparing for the Term

Whether you are reading this training guide three months, three weeks, or three days prior to the start of the semester, you want to be well prepared to guide students through public speaking as a learning experience. Concerning your own version of the course, you may be experiencing many of the same feelings that your students will before their speeches. The questions are relatively simple:

- What is my role as the instructor in this particular course?

- What text should I use and how can I use it most effectively?

- How should I structure the course?

- What class policies should I establish?

- How do I build a good syllabus?

You must work out the detailed answers to these questions, but the following discussion offers some starting points and coordinates to help you prepare for the term ahead and frame the course to accomplish your instructional objectives.

The Roles of the Instructor in the Course

You will wear many instructional hats while teaching public speaking—more than in conventional college courses. Like conventional courses, you are responsible for course content and classroom management, examinations and assignments. In addition to these regular responsibilities, public speaking also includes performance components that:

- Link student success in the course more directly to the instructor;

- Raise performance expectations for the instructor as a speaker;

- Include the dual roles of coach and judge on the instructor.

Negotiating your multiple roles as the classroom instructor will be a continuing process in public speaking. Students will benefit as you gain the skill and will to manage your roles and to clarify your roles for students. As mentioned earlier, most public speaking courses cover the classroom material in approximately one-half of the class meetings to allow time for student speaking performances. Within the limited time for conventional instruction, students seem to benefit from a combination of exercises, discussion, and lecture. While lectures might cover the material most efficiently, instructional effectiveness may suffer if you make lectures the predominant instructional method. Because performance issues permeate the course, public speaking puts you in unique instructional roles with which many students may be unaccustomed, therefore they deserve our attention.

Demands of Instructing a Performance Course

The performance aspect of the public speaking course is a wild card for students. A student could receive 100 percent of the points available on every written assignment including exams and only manage a *B* in public speaking. And this is as it should be, despite the fact that highly-literate, grade-conscious students often object to the arrangement. More points *should* be dedicated to speeches than any other activity. Therefore, students who perform poorly in their speeches may receive lower grades than they do in other courses. Such occurrences are rare, but you will occasionally encounter students who believe that mastery of course material demonstrated on written assignments should translate into positive performance evaluations, even though their speeches are mediocre. You will also have students who invest hours of work on a five-minute speech that completely flops. They may expect a higher mark based on their effort. Students want classes to prepare them for the "real world," but they may not like your methods of preparation. The real world is a place where performance counts—where clients or bosses or customers or constituents never see the preparation, only the actual performance—and people make judgments on the quality of the presentation alone. The public speaking classroom is rarely as harsh, arbitrary, or vindictive as the real world, even when we do take performance seriously.

Students may believe that you ask them to do too much and then grade them too subjectively. Because the course demands that they develop new cognitive skills and communication practices, they *should* feel like you are asking them to do too much at once. Although you will have a grading system that focuses on objectively observable behaviors and components in their speeches, they may initially have the sense that you are grading them in a subjective, arbitrary manner—especially if they believe they deserve a higher grade than they receive. The fact of performance and the evaluation of performance put you in a different situation than courses with no performance component, and these aspects permeate the entire course. But the course also places unique performance demands on you as the instructor that students will recognize almost immediately and that needs to be managed with poise and agility.

Instructor-Student Relationship and Student Experience

Your classroom presence, priorities, and practices will be the dominant factor in students' experience of the public speaking course. Based on my own interaction with many instructors, students, and course directors, the instructor seems to play the crucial role in public speaking student learning. *Because of their instructors,* many students come to enjoy the course despite the anxiety attached to giving speeches. On the other hand, some students who could learn the material and excel in performance suffer through the course *because of their instructors.* The nature of the course and the experience of course directors suggests that the instructional connection between teacher and student is a more significant factor in public speaking classes than it may be in others. As a result, I tell students that they should transfer to another section of the course or drop the course so that they can take it from a different instructor if they suspect that we might have problems working together in the classroom. But in most cases, preparation for your different roles and advance explanation of your roles for students can enhance the learning experience for a great majority of students who come to your class.

Dynamics of Dual Roles: Instructor and Performer

As you have probably anticipated, your role as a performer in the classroom will be accentuated. As public speaking teachers, we need to practice what we preach. Composition teachers do not ordinarily submit their own writing for student scrutiny, but students will immediately get a sense for your speaking skills. If you have extensive speaking experience, the performance factor should be relatively comfortable and your thoughts may turn to how you can utilize your own experience most effectively in the classroom context. However, if you have limited speaking experience or have never been trained in public speaking through a college course or professional seminar, the prospect can be intimidating. But you need not be an accomplished presenter to teach this course well. Use the course to learn the material and use the classroom to practice the skills your students will need to perform. You can transfer the performance skills you develop while teaching public speaking to every other course you eventually teach. Many aspects of effective pedagogical communication parallel the ideas and skills you will teach in public speaking, so concentrate on improving your own performances in class. You will benefit, and so will your students.

Dynamics of Dual Roles: Coach and Judge

Grading the performance of students whom you have taught raises a dilemma. You must play the dual roles of coach and judge. An Olympic ice skating coach invests hours, days, weeks, months, and years teaching skating. Then, when the competition begins, the coach prepares the skater to handle the situation and encourages the athlete to deliver a peak performance. Someone else judges the performance. As a public speaking instructor, like a coach or trainer, you will teach students the concepts and skills expected to be enacted in their speeches. You will want them to do well. However, just when your students are ready to "step onto the ice," you will have to take to the judges' stand and evaluate their performances as impartially as possible.

Many instructors struggle with this paradox. The difficulties associated with the dual role of coach and judge surround three main issues:

1. How do performances reflect teaching effectiveness?

2. How will this grade affect future performances?

3. How will the student respond to me as a teacher if I give this grade?

None of these questions has an easy answer, but in each case new instructors are susceptible to contributing to grade inflation by following the path of least resistance. Let me explain.

First, do not use student performances—strong or weak—as a gauge of instructional effectiveness. A novice's performance cannot be reduced to instruction alone. Apprehension (especially in early speaking rounds), inadequate preparation, romance lost or found, an exam in another class the same day, or any number of other factors may contribute to a poor performance. Therefore, your evaluation should not be tempered in favor of the student because they did not execute what you taught. To do so assumes a pedagogical failure. Your evaluation scheme should reflect the concepts and skills you have emphasized in class. Explain the evaluation form clearly and indicate the standards for grade ranges in advance. Over the entire course, your teaching will play a significant role in student development. But the connections between teaching and particular performances are varied, indirect, and quite dependent on each student's particular level of engagement in the course. If you see a pattern in which the majority of students omit something you thought you had taught clearly, maintain the same standard throughout the speaking round and make adjustments before the next set of speeches.

Second, vow to yourself never to use a grade as a motivation tool, positively or negatively. Some teachers purposely grade the first round of speeches low—no one gets above a *B*. These instructors believe that their students rise to the challenge and make greater improvement through the term if their first performance is judged harshly. Most new instructors take the opposite tack. They fear that students will be discouraged by a low grade. In these cases, an *F* becomes a *C*, a *D* becomes a *B*, a *C* becomes an *A-*, a *B* becomes an *A*, and an *A* becomes an *A+*. Use written comments and suggestions as motivators, not grades. Practice saying, "You got a high mark on this speech, but you have a number of ways to improve," and "Your evaluation was low because of these factors in the speech, but you can address them by . . ." Instructors have neither the power to degrade nor to elevate anyone's self-esteem through a single speech grade. But you can mislead, which could give a student an inaccurate impression about their level of performance that could harm them in the future.

Third, resist the temptation to curry favor or "buy" good teaching evaluations with speech grades. Beginning teachers commonly succumb to the desire for student approval. Giving slightly higher grades where possible seems to be a good way to win favor. The reasoning on teaching evaluations follows a simple syllogistic pattern: teaching evaluations correlate directly with expected grades in the course (the higher the grades, the higher the teaching evaluations); I will make sure that everyone who comes to class and tries in this course receives an *A* or a *B*; I will receive favorable teaching evaluations. The syllogism breaks down in the initial premise. The correlation between grades and teaching evaluation is a contested question. Furthermore, reflect on your best, most highly respected teachers. Do you rate them primarily based on the grades you earned in their class?

In summary, you need to prepare yourself and your students for the different roles you will need to play through the term, especially the ones associated with performance aspects of the course. Articulate the roles that you are playing as the course develops. By doing so, you will enable students to adjust their expectations and you will help them to maximize their learning experience. Recognize the impact of your classroom presence on the quality of student experiences in the course overall, own your responsibility to practice what you preach in class, and make the distinctions between your dual roles as coach and judge clear, without compromising either one.

Incorporating Your Textbook into the Course

You experienced a variety of uses for textbooks in your college career (some of which had no connection to the course you were taking). Try to remember cases in which a textbook that enhanced your learning experience was neglected by your professor. There may be a few.

But in most cases, the effectiveness of the textbook can be linked to the instructor's active use of the text in the class. How do you expect students to use the book? Will you expect them to bring their books to each class meeting? If you ask them to, will they continue to do so because of your regular use of the text as a learning tool? What can you do to help students to utilize the book seriously, not just read it the night before a test?

The Role of the Text in the Course

When you begin to teach public speaking, the textbook will be one of the most important components in your regimen. You know why the textbook is important to you. One of your main tasks is deciding how the textbook will become important to your students. As you know, college instructors tend not to cover the text in detail during class sessions. First, most college instructors design a course to reflect their personal knowledge and experience in the subject. Second, between their own knowledge, the text, other material, and the time constraints of the course, no one could cover the territory comprehensively in class alone. Finally, college courses include the expectation that students gain much of their knowledge outside of class time. While this should make the text more important to students, they will not take the text seriously unless you do. No one but you can define the role of the text in your class. Students will value the text depending upon your expectations for them to rely on the text in class sessions, assignments, and exams.

Following are some ideas about roles that the text can play in a student's learning experience. I suggest that you try them all initially, discarding only those which seem to you to be fruitless after three or more semesters.

Expect Pre-class Preparation

Students will learn more if you prime their mental pumps by expecting them to work with textbook material prior to coming to class. Some instructors quiz regularly to keep students up to speed. Others assign one or two discussion questions to be submitted for minimal credit (perhaps "participation") for each reading assignment. The latter approach seems superior in the sense that the discussion can be incorporated into the class session, thereby encouraging students to integrate their reading with the material introduced in class. Quizzes tend to get students focused on the text as a source of points, which the student mind unreflectively stores in short-term memory (i.e. not to be learned). Discussion questions collected at the beginning of the class are one way to get students to read without nagging them.

Textbook as a Source of Activities and Exercises

If students work with the textbook in class they will value it more and learn more from it outside of class. Quality textbooks incorporate a variety of activities and exercises from which to select. You should receive a desk copy with special notes for instructors and an instructor's manual that includes additional activities, exercises, and assignments. Choose activities from the text that effectively reinforce class concepts. Many texts also include "special feature" segments within the regular text that highlight their emphases—these too can be used as discussion points.

Sample Speeches in the Textbook

From antiquity, public speaking teachers have recognized that models help students learn the concepts and strategies necessary to excel. Because speaking is a performance, examples of the concepts and skills taught in the course are particularly helpful and plentiful. Textbooks broaden the scope of examples. Most include a variety of student speeches and noteworthy public speeches. Allyn & Bacon offers a fine DVD of *Classic and Contemporary Speeches,* a video anthology of American speeches from the past century to support its public speaking textbooks [suggestions for how to use *Classic and Contemporary Speeches* will be included throughout this guide]. No student will connect with every example in class or in the book, so a wide assortment serves to enhance learning opportunities. Examples can be used for discussion and as case studies.

The Textbook as a Speaker's Reference

Student appreciation for the textbook may grow as their graded speech assignments approach. What initially may seem dry and difficult reading can come to life as they are planning their own speech. Give them reminders. In your written evaluations, prescribe particular sections of the text, even specific pages, to help them improve on the weaknesses you diagnose in their early speeches.

In the public speaking course, you will be the most important source of information and direction for your students, but a well-employed textbook can enhance student learning by supplementing and reinforcing the objectives and content of your course.

Supplementing the Text

As you approach the first round of student speeches, you may want to show a sample student speech—an example of a peer performing well. Perhaps you want to inspire your students by exposing them to an exemplary speech by a popular figure. Allyn & Bacon's *Classic and Contemporary Speeches* DVD includes a number of favorites like JFK's speech at the Berlin Wall, MLK, Jr.'s "I Have a Dream," and Ronald Reagan's speech after the Challenger disaster. Perhaps you want students to use speech design software or learn effective use of the Internet for research. All of these cases can be addressed through supplemental resources. You might be able to find supplements like the ones mentioned above by conducting a search personally. But quality textbooks today include a wide range of supplemental materials designed to complement your course. Most items are provided at no charge; others are available for a modest fee. For students, you may elect to include speech design software, speech planning workbooks, Internet use for speech research guides, etc. Allyn & Bacon provides a complete spectrum of supplements for teachers and students. In the final chapter of this training manual you will find a matrix connecting these supplements with the appropriate chapters of Allyn & Bacon's public speaking textbooks.

You may also choose to supplement the textbook with a variety of handouts, including speech texts from the past (recent and distant) or worksheets of your own design. Providing working handouts that encourage students to develop their speech ideas as you proceed through the conceptual material in the course will help them to stay engaged with the material you are teaching. I personally recommend that you select or develop a speech evaluation form [a sample form is included in Chapter Four of this guide] and attempt to plan your major assignments in advance with assignment sheets for students. If you can combine your handouts, assignment sheets, and evaluation forms into a packet that can be purchased inexpensively from your department office or at the campus bookstore(s), you will provide a valuable supplemental resource for your students and save yourself much time and energy at the copy machine during the term.

Structuring the Course

You have the foundation set for your course. You should possess a sense of how your version of public speaking fits in your community. Your teaching objectives are set and you have positioned the textbook and supplements to resonate with your instructional plan. Now you must establish a structure to make your version of the course a concrete learning experience for you and your students. Use the syllabus as a tool to develop that structure. If you are working within a standard syllabus for the course, review the syllabus and master these elements *before* the course begins, reflecting on how you will implement them in your particular classroom.

Strategic Development of the Syllabus

Think of your syllabus as a blueprint or owner's manual for the course. No one should be forced to read one in its entirety (many students do not anyway), but each of the particulars may become crucial to the effectiveness of a larger project in its own time. As the person in charge of running the course, you should always be able to see the whole in relationship to each part. As you develop or work through the syllabus, make sure that the agenda it sets reflects your expectations for students and your commitments to the course. The syllabus also should be a realistic rendering of what is possible regarding instruction. Likewise, the policies contained in it should be enforceable and aimed at enhancing performance rather than entrapment and retribution.

Number of Class Sessions in the Term

The first reality check of your instructional aspirations should come as you reflect on the number and length of the class sessions in the term. Face the fact that, whether you are teaching a semester, quarter, summer term, degree-completion program, or any other format, you simply will not have enough time. Once you have adjusted to the fundamental limitation of time, the configuration of your term still makes a significant difference. Regardless of the type of term, you still must provide students with instruction and performance opportunities. But how you do this and how the term structure affects student learning will vary widely. Will your students be taking four to five other courses simultaneously? How close will their first, second, and third speeches be to one another in time? Will a speaking round last two weeks or two days? Will a speaking round last two class sessions or six? How will you divide instructional time? You should address these issues and factors as you prepare your course calendar. Expect the process of developing the calendar to involve a good deal of juggling and compromise before you arrive at a workable arrangement.

Framework for Performance and Evaluation

Public speaking teachers must make compromises in developing a course calendar because approximately one-half of class sessions are ordinarily devoted to graded student speech performances. You may include other, non-graded speaking exercises or activities as well. Therefore, instructional time is precious. The performance aspect of the course puts unique pressures on class sessions and adds significant dimensions to evaluation in the course.

The syllabus frames the role of instruction, speech performances, and evaluation via speech grading and exams. I understand that some instructors choose to divide the term in half, front-loading all of the traditional classroom instruction in the first half of the term and then using the second half of the term for student speeches. Ordinarily, teachers choose to take a more incremental approach, introducing basic skills and working up to the more sophisticated aspects of speech design, reasoning, argumentation, and presentation as the term progresses. Therefore, if you are building your own syllabus, you need to make choices about what to include and where in the course to insert each instructional segment .

- How many speeches and of what type will you require?

- Will you include some instruction on ceremonial speaking and on serving as a master of ceremonies?

- How much time will you allot for each student's speech, including time you allow for peer feedback and your comments?

- Will you include a visit to the campus library?

- Do you expect to incorporate instruction on group presentations?

- Do you intend to show videos of student speeches and famous speakers?

- Will you devote time to impromptu speaking?

- How many exams or quizzes will you include?

Finally, consider how your course fits with the rest of your responsibilities—other courses you may be teaching or taking, other employment, or personal plans and commitments. Remember that whatever you assign must also be graded, so consider how much time the course will require. For instance, if you have not graded speeches before you should probably allow about 15-20 minutes per speech.

Structure for Grading Performance

If possible within the constraints of your course, incorporate strategies that help you and your students prepare for speech grading. The strategies I suggest enable students to have some authentic performance experience in your classroom before the first graded speeches, provide you with a "dry run" on grading, and allow you to establish expectations for how you will be grading and commenting on speeches.

1. Distribute speech evaluation criteria with your syllabus, course packet, or as a handout early in the course. (See sample at the end of the chapter.)

2. Connect impromptu speeches and other speaking exercises to focus student attention on elements of speaking that you will be evaluating in their graded speeches. Within the context of such exercises, explain the evaluation criteria and examples of different levels of performance.

3. Assign a short, introductory speech early in the term. Do not count the speech for a grade. Have students videotape their speeches. Provide written feedback and indicate the grade that would have been achieved.

Course Policies

Establish expectations for key elements of the course in the syllabus. A special section devoted to "course policies" can help you to avoid difficulties during the term. In public speaking classes, attendance, grading, cheating, and access to the instructor are all major factors to consider. You may have other policies or issues within your particular course. Set parameters and policies clearly in writing and reinforce your policies in class at the beginning of the term. Students rarely respond favorably to mid-course changes or late introduction of policies.

Attendance

Full participation by all students in every class session makes a big difference in the vitality of the learning process in public speaking. Make attendance mandatory unless you can come up with strong rationale for letting students come and go as they please. Why? Without the mandate, certain students will routinely miss the learning opportunities available during speaking rounds because "they're only giving speeches today." Some of the most important learning in a public speaking course should be happening during student speeches. But absences, particularly by students who have already presented their speeches, detract from the classroom environment for other speakers and generally sap energy from the course.

Some instructors make attendance mandatory, but tell students that they may miss two to three class sessions without penalty. Acknowledging to yourself that students may not be able to make each and every class meeting is realistic; however, I recommend that the grace applied to the first few absences not be announced publicly but merely figured at the end of the course. If you allow for two or three "personal days," students will use them and may expect more leniency in general. Expect your students to communicate with you every time they miss class. Do not count legitimate absences, but do penalize frivolous ones. Using language such as, "You should *expect* absences to have a negative impact on your grade," gives you flexibility to apply the attendance policy fairly, but sends the message that students should be in every class possible.

Grading System

To call grades a preoccupation with students severely understates the case. At some point in the term, most students are likely to review this segment of the syllabus to check their status in the course. Your grading scale, the values assigned to each assignment, and how you handle late work, extra credit, and complaints will be scrutinized by many students every term. Therefore, review each of the following areas and any other grade-related issues presented by your course. Most colleges and universities use a standard grading scale. If one exists, use it. If not, determine the predominant grading scale that students encounter and incorporate it if possible.

Establishing Assignment Values. The values you assign to each assignment—how you balance speeches, exams, exercises, etc., will be more important than the grading scale you list. First, give priority to assigning the largest proportion of points to speeches. In certain exceptional cases, an instructor might justify assigning a larger proportion of credit to other elements of the course than to the total amount of points available for speeches. However, speeches should ordinarily make up at least 40 percent of the total points and, when combined with specific speech preparation and evaluation, assignments might reach 60 to 70 percent of credit for the course. Second, do not cave in to the feeling some instructors get that students will only do assignments worth points. Save your points for substantial exercises, exams, papers, and speeches. If you want students to do class preparation work for which they receive no credit, provide the rationale for the work. Find ways to reward people who participate, like including the work in examination material or providing helpful feedback on the assignment only to participants. I recommend that you stick to a 1,000-point scale and break your evaluations into five-point increments whenever possible, especially on exams. Make test items worth at least five points and then use factors of five. By doing so, you make clear distinctions between grades, resist the temptation to award discretionary points, and suppress the inclination of some students to argue over a single point.

Speeches: Equal or Incremental? On speech grades specifically, two options are popular. You can value each speech equally, assuming that skill development is incremental. The first speech is worth as much as the last (or roughly so) because a great deal had to be learned to accomplish the first, whereas every speech afterward takes the earlier learning for granted. The value is assigned according to the additional skills and concepts attending the later speeches. On the other hand, you can create an ascending point value for each speech, assuming that students should be given time to mature as speakers. The first evaluated speech should be "safe" so that doing poorly as an inexperienced speaker does not disqualify students from achieving high marks for the course. Either choice can work effectively, depending on how the instructor handles each one. In general, the former encourages students to take the early speeches more seriously, and the latter tends to be more conducive to grade inflation.

Late Work and Extra Credit. In addition to these grading basics, your syllabus should reflect your policies on late work and extra credit. When is work considered "late?" *If I ask for an extension, should I expect a point deduction, or does my request negate any penalty?* I recommend that you establish a standard, workable policy for late work. Some instructors use a scale of diminishing points depending on how late the work is submitted. Others establish a standard percentage deduction. For speeches, you need to consider whether you will permit students to make up speeches that they skip and, if so, what penalty you will apply to a late speech. You should also set the process for making up speeches in advance, and make-ups should never compromise the quality of the learning experience for students who are prepared to speak on time.

What about extra credit? *If I discover I am doing poorly at the end of your course, can I get a personal assignment of extra work to make up the difference and keep my grade point average up?* In many cases, colleagues or graduate students will want you to offer extra credit as an incentive for students to participate as research subjects. Will all students be permitted to participate? If not, what alternative extra credit options will you provide for those not selected for a study or who cannot participate due to other constraints? *How much extra credit could I possibly get as a student? If I end the course with a 70 percent based on the merits of the regular work, how high can my grade ascend?* I recommend that you not allow extra credit to move any student more than four percent above the level they earn through the usual work in public speaking. This approach gives students an opportunity to move from a low grade in a range to a higher version of the same grade, or they can move from the top of one range to the bottom of another, but no more than that.

Grade Complaint Policy. A syllabus that outlines a process for managing grade complaints in public speaking will protect you from frivolous grade complaints at the end of the semester. *I need to get the _____ to: get into this major or social organization; keep my scholarship; remain eligible.* A good grade complaint policy should include at least the following elements:

1. **Do not discuss a grade immediately after the student receives it.** Require the students to take time (at least 24 hours) to reflect on their performance and your evaluation, not just react to the disparity between their grades and their expectations.

2. **Do not discuss grades in the classroom or in the hall.** Reserve such discussions for appointments. By doing so you protect the student's confidentiality and avoid the expansion of a personal matter to the class as a whole. A grade is only the business of the instructor and the concerned student.

3. **Establish a statute of limitations (1-2 weeks) after which assignment grades (speeches, exams, papers, etc.) will not be reviewed.** If a student is concerned

about a grade on its own merits rather than how it detracts from the desired GPA, then she or he will make a point of speaking with you about it soon after the grade is assigned. Otherwise, disappointed students tend to choose grades on which they believe they can make the best case, not because they objected originally, but because as the consequences of their performance begin to materialize they want points to improve their grades at the last minute.

4. **Demand that all evaluated materials be brought to a grade appeal meeting.** Documentation helps you and the student. You need to review the bases on which you assigned the grade. Also, you could be mistaken, whether mathematically or in the substance of your evaluation. But you have to be able to see it to make that assessment.

5. **Require that the grade appeal be put in writing.** This benefits the student as well as you. First, the work involved in writing the appeal discourages complaints without merit. Second, the written appeal allows the student to think through her/his case and present it clearly, which can be difficult to do when attempting to launch the appeal in a one-on-one conversation. Finally, you get an opportunity to hear the complaint as a whole. The written complaint limits the scope of the discussion and can help to bring it to a satisfactory resolution more swiftly.

While the above suggestions are applicable to a variety of courses, they are especially pertinent to public speaking. Instructors and students alike understand the necessarily subjective aspects of evaluating speech performances. Clarifying your grade appeal process makes grade complaints a much more serious matter for students, deflecting frivolous complaints and averting personal embarrassment for some. By taking the initiative, you redirect the purpose of reviewing student concerns and put yourself in the position to either retain or revise your initial judgment, but to maintain a high level of respect with the student, regardless. As a good friend of mine was fond of saying to students, "I spent 30 minutes listening to and evaluating your speech. I expect the same kind of investment from you if you want me to reconsider. Surely, you don't think I'd forsake all that work and overturn it in a moment without full documentation and a careful review!"

Academic Integrity

In most institutions, public speaking presents special challenges in the area of academic integrity. Many sections of the course are offered each semester, which means that material from the course is widely available. Students find the prospect of giving a speech nerve-wracking, and so may be more severely tempted to violate ethical standards in the process of getting help. Stories are legion of speech files maintained by fraternities, sororities, and other social organizations to save time and produce grades for members. More recently, Internet sites reportedly provide "canned" speeches on assorted topics to help students cut corners and meet standards. Less legendary, but perhaps more common are groups of students taking the course in different sections during the same term trying to economize on labor by collaborating on research, organization, visual aids, and more.

Learn the Campus Policy. Familiarize yourself with the stated policy of your college or university on academic integrity. Your syllabus should identify the course with these standards. Then you must define what the general standards mean in your version of the public speaking course.

- What constitutes plagiarism in a speech?

- Can students work together on any aspect of research or speech design?

- Can previous work be used in your class?

While you are reviewing the institutional policies and definitions, review the procedure you should follow if you suspect an infraction against academic integrity. If someone is cheating in your class, you want to know the first move and what sorts of options you possess.

Prevention or Policing. The most important decision to consider is how you will orient yourself and the course toward the possibility for infractions, which occur every term in at least some sections of the course. Obviously, you could simply choose to devote no attention to the reality of cheating and other violations in your class. Few instructors exercise this option. Practically, you have two clear emphases from which to choose: either structure the course assignments to make cheating difficult and unlikely to produce the desired result (a better grade) or structure the course to enable you to identify and document instances of cheating easily. Please consider where you want to expend your primary instructional energy and proceed accordingly.

Definitions and References. In either case, students should know your definitions and expectations regarding academic integrity by reading your course policies. Picture yourself reviewing the policy with someone who has committed an infraction. They should be feeling intensely foolish, with no way to weasel out, whether they collaborated, plagiarized, or violated the policy in some other way. Also, make sure that you refer to the policies and give examples in class the first day and at other appropriate times through the semester. Note in your grade book and lesson plans the class sessions in which you spoke about academic integrity.

You must note the times you speak about academic integrity in class along with stating your policy in the syllabus to document that you do, in fact, take academic integrity seriously. Some students will claim that they did not understand the policy and could not have been expected to because of instructor negligence.

Dealing with Suspicions. Two situations regarding academic integrity can be particularly challenging. In one case, you have strong suspicions that someone has not done their own work. In the other, you have caught someone and must determine how to proceed.

Occasionally, a student submits work that does not match their ordinary level of performance or in some other way suggests to you that the student has not done the work alone. The student apparently has stolen the work, purchased it, or inappropriately collaborated with others. But you have no way to document or prove this fact. The most effective way to combat this sort of infraction is through prevention.

Structure your assignments so that any work done by someone outside of the course would be substandard. In most cases, the product of the infraction will be off-target in both form and content. Even in a course in which the assignments are specified by the department or a course director, you can usually add a few wrinkles as the classroom instructor that will preserve the integrity of the assignment while revealing a lack of integrity in the cheating student that you grade appropriately. Do not miss an opportunity to remark on the high general quality of the work and the sad fact that it grades low because it neglects key elements of the assignment.

In the second case, you must decide how to proceed with a violation that you can prove. A multitude of dynamics surface in such situations, and no textbook can provide the most important information you need to accomplish the greatest good for the institution and the person involved. But do consider this one issue. If you decide that the matter does not rise to the level of official sanction (failure for the course, expulsion, etc.), you may still draft a letter regarding the infraction to be placed on file with the chair of the department as a probationary step. Such a letter does not become part of the student's official file and will not be forwarded beyond the department *unless* a second infraction comes to light. In other words, you document the offense in a kind of institutional short-term memory. If the student operates with integrity, the record disappears upon graduation. If the student repeats the behavior, the record emerges publicly for consideration in connection with later violations.

Dealing with Infractions. Follow the process outlined in your school's code of ethics, student handbook, or the equivalent. In addition, consider each of the following when you meet with a student concerning an academic integrity infraction:

1. Do not meet with the student alone. Include the course director, a faculty member, or another instructor who teaches the same course in the meeting.

2. Every time you meet with a student about possible infractions document the meeting and its outcome. If the decisions you make are ever appealed or challenged, you will need a paper trail.

3. Weigh the consequence for the infraction carefully. In most institutions, you will determine the penalty. Avoid playing the merciless champion appointed to save the corrupted academy. On the other hand, the process of prosecution for cheating or other violation is not, in itself, a sufficient consequence. The second chance most students need comes by assisting them in negotiating the severe difficulties that should attend cheating, not in premature absolution.

Accessibility

Think about the times and places students are likely to be able to meet with you. Then review your schedule to determine your time commitments and how your free moments match up with opportunities to meet with students. If you can, find times when your students can meet with you conveniently and in which you are unlikely to be able to get much work done anyway. In some cases, you may choose to meet students for office hours in a context other than your office. For example, you might find a quiet spot in a coffee shop or other comfortable meeting place on campus. Also, determine how you will make yourself accessible to students via telephone and e-mail.

Ordinarily, students should be able to reach you by phone and e-mail and you should be prepared to respond. However, whether students should have access to your *home* phone or other off-campus numbers and what they should expect concerning e-mail are negotiable. Take into account the nature of the course, the size of the class, campus culture, any departmental or institutional guidelines, and relevant aspects of your work life and home life outside of class as you consider these basic questions:

- What contact options should I provide (office, home, cell phone, e-mail)?

- When should students be encouraged/discouraged to call?

- What minimum/maximum e-mail response time should I tell students to expect?

Also, consider establishing a *course Web page*. If you know how to design one, or have assistance available on campus to create such a Web page, you can create a mailbox on the Web page for personal e-mail correspondence related to class that does not involve your personal e-mail account. For those skilled in Web-based application, a Web page can also integrate conventional classroom components with some of the benefits of online instruction, including simple means to organize and work with electronic submission of assignments, out-of-class discussions, etc.

Finalizing the Syllabus

At this point you have thought through everything from your role as an instructor to determining when and how students can contact you outside of class. If you use the elements of the syllabus to guide your planning and the structure for the course, when it comes to writing the syllabus you will have only to plug in the various components. Complete the syllabus segments in reverse order, as follows:

1. Set your course calendar and include reading due dates and major assignment due dates. Students may not refer to the calendar frequently, but when they do, they will know what is happening.

2. As you determine how to incorporate the major assignments, write a brief description of each assignment and your exam format(s).

3. Formalize your course policies in writing, explaining attendance and participation expectations, grading, and academic integrity issues.

4. Write a statement on why students should take public speaking and your objectives.

5. Provide contact information and guidelines to set expectations for student access to you as an instructor. This should include office hours, phone number(s), e-mail address, or Web page URL.

When you finish the syllabus, it should proceed from contact information, to objectives, through course policies and major assignments, which finally take shape in the concrete dates and assignments in the course calendar.

Many challenges and opportunities will arise impromptu during the term—things that we can never account for in a syllabus. However, the process of working through the issues, challenges, and opportunities necessary to build a solid syllabus will put you in the best position to negotiate the unanticipated to the best advantage of the learning process for you and your public speaking students.

SPEECH EVALUATION GUIDELINES

These guidelines are provided to help students understand grade ranges for speech assignments. Specific criteria will vary from section to section, but will be applied consistently *within* your section, based on in-class instruction and the requirements for each speech. *(Consider these ranges while referring to the specific speech assignment pages and evaluation forms in your course workbook.)*

A Range　　SUPERIOR. You developed a creative, imaginative, original approach to the entire assignment AND showed mastery in each required category for the assignment with distinction. *(In the real world, this is what professional quality speeches ought to be, but rarely are. You should be paid for this speech.)*

B Range　　EXCELLENT. You exceeded all of the minimum written standards for the assignment, showing ingenuity and resourcefulness in both the development and the performance of the speech. *(In the real world, this is an excellent amateur speech, and better than most professional speeches. You should receive genuine, enthusiastic applause and good questions at the conclusion of this speech.)*

C Range　　COMPETENT. You met the minimum written standards for the assignment. *(In the real world, this is a good speech, and the average speech you're likely to hear in the workplace. You should receive applause with handshakes, congratulations, and a few good questions at the conclusion of this speech.)*

D Range　　DEFICIENT. You gave a speech, but did not meet the minimum standards for the assignment due to some serious flaw or omission. *(In the real world, there are speeches like this given every day by professionals who need to take a public speaking course like this one. They do not advance knowledge, business, the common good, or their own careers. You will receive undeserved applause for the sake of common courtesy. Questions will be asked, but not of you.)*
   a.　　You read your speech (from a manuscript or note cards).
   b.　　You gave evidence of memorizing your speech.
   c.　　You performed unsatisfactorily on a combination of categories.
   d.　　You experienced a critical breakdown in organization, support, structure, or delivery.
   e.　　You neglected your audience, either in adaptation of the message to them or in your ethical responsibility to them.

F Range　　FAILURE. You experienced a comprehensive, catastrophic breakdown on the assignment.
   a.　　Did not present your speech. (No credit)
   b.　　Chose to do a speech project other than the one assigned (e.g., a speech to entertain).
   c.　　Attempted a speech, but performed unsatisfactorily in all categories.

For any act of academic misconduct during the preparation or performance of the project (including the outline or other related participation assignments) you may fail the entire course. (See the workbook and university's Student Handbook.) Every speech must be developed and designed by you independently—no assistance from others except as directed expressly by the instructor.

RATIONALE: These standards—specifically geared toward college-level speakers—are designed to motivate you to learn how to give a professional-quality presentation under better-than-workplace conditions. *We want you to achieve excellence, not competence!* (Each will be rewarded accordingly within the grade ranges above.)

Chapter Three:
Putting the Plan into Action

You have framed your version of public speaking. Now you must prepare to take it into the classroom. Recall that most of your students will come to the course with little experience and less training. You should be able to envision what will happen through the term, including many of the learning challenges, possibilities, and opportunities presented by the course. Your students may be enthusiastic, skeptical, or fearful, but they will all be uncertain about what lies ahead for them when they walk into your class. They will probably have little to go on beyond rumors, hopes, and fears. Even experienced speakers may have anxiety about a course in which you will evaluate their speaking skill and they will be exposed to the scrutiny of their peers simultaneously.

Teaching Coordinates for the Basic Public Speaking Course

When you enter your classroom as an instructor, you have the burden and privilege of possessing knowledge of public speaking theory and practice that your students have not yet learned. The substance to which you will introduce students is not merely personal; you have the support of the discipline and your colleagues with you in each class session. You are more than a mere facilitator—although you will have done well if you successfully facilitate learning through the entire term. You are also more than just a manager—although how you manage the course and the classroom will affect the learning process profoundly. To teach well, you must be a visionary intent on inviting students into a new level of knowledge and practice about human communication. Your students may harbor some concerns about negotiating the course well. Therefore, you need both to envision the course as a whole and to lead students into a concrete, day-by-day learning experience that will seem adventurous to student and teacher alike.

Cultivating a Healthy Learning Environment

Think about this question: What do college professors do (or fail to do) that stifles a learning climate or disrupts the classroom environment? Take a few moments to list specific behaviors that you have seen in college classrooms. Then consider the positive side of the same issue: What makes a classroom a good learning environment? How can you establish a climate that will help students to accomplish the learning objectives you have established for public speaking? Obviously, the instructor sets the tone. The climate should correspond to the content and style in the course. In particular, the classroom should promote interaction. You should make it a safe place—one where people can voice their opinions in a respectful community, without fear of personal attack (from the instructor or classmates!). Students should know that they can make occasional delivery errors without severe consequences and should leave the course with a better sense of freedom of speech than when the term began. At the same time, you want students to recognize the need for them to engage fully in the course material and class sessions. They should find a certain intensity and dynamism for learning every time they come to class.

Adapting to Students

The sheer volume of concepts, theories, and skills deployed in the course are of little consequence to students. Therefore, our chief concern should be what the student needs to know, understand, and do. The means to accomplish this goal resides in connecting with their existing world of experience and knowledge. Forsake visions of pretentious instructors adopting current student attitudes, wardrobe, jargon, etc. Adapting the course material to students can be accomplished in more pedestrian ways, which make the methods more effective.

Here are a few ways to get started adapting the course content to your particular classes:

1. **Begin with What Students Already Know:** Students know a great deal about public speaking; they simply lack coordinates and categories to make sense of their knowledge. Start from their context and their terms whenever possible, then move them toward the next order of thinking.

2. **Connect New Material Directly to Course Assignments:** Tie each class meeting to a project on which they are currently working. Help them to see the conceptual connections to their assignment. Do not automatically assume that they will see the relationships. Keep them working on their speech projects and committing, during class time, to choices about how to proceed.

3. **Model the Speech Design Process:** Work through a sample topic of your own for each speech assignment. By your example and your working with them through the new concepts, they will learn much about your expectations for things like narrowing

their topics and adequately supporting their points. Avoid using overly abstract or simplistic topics as hypothetical cases.

Public Speaking in a Second Language

Language skills play a decisive role in public speaking courses. Many courses may have students who are not native English speakers. On some campuses, students' first languages may vary widely. As people skilled in ESL (English as a Second Language) know, speaking in a second language is much more difficult than understanding the spoken language, and can also present much greater challenges than writing in a second language. If native speakers have speech apprehension, imagine what a first semester international student may feel during the early days of a required public speaking course!

Instructors need to approach such situations with great care. Remember that the public speaking course not only demands sophisticated oral skill from all students, but the course itself is also deeply grounded in American democratic culture. ESL students may struggle as much with cultural issues regarding public speaking as they do with the immediate issues of fluency in English. Plan to deal with each student personally and extend yourself by making contact with colleagues in your institution who teach and study ESL issues. Also, you might consider ordering *ESL Guide for Public Speaking* by Debra Gonsher Vinik, published by Allyn & Bacon. The guide provides strategies, suggestions, and additional resources for ESL in the public speaking classroom.

Finally, note that through a supportive environment for ESL, many non-native English speaking students will make rapid progress in their public fluency as a direct result of merely being forced to use their English in the public speaking classroom.

Modeling Presentation Skills

Beginning instructors in public speaking tend to feel pressure to perform—literally to practice what they are preaching. We know that students benefit from a good model. However, sticking to a view of students as prospective speakers alone may not be the most helpful approach for teachers. Instead, think about a different question: What challenges do undergraduates face *as listeners* in a public speaking classroom?

Moving students from a mistake-free performance orientation to one grounded in listener needs should guide your own class presentations. In other words, should speakers simply try to make an impression, or do they actually have something of substance to communicate? If communication is the goal, then you can take initiative in a number of ways that can improve connections between instructors and students.

Room Arrangement and Proximity

If the room in which you teach has movable seating, consider adjusting the seating arrangement to enhance interaction and keep students in closer proximity to you and one another. Semi-circular or U-shaped arrangements are particularly effective, even if they need to be two rows deep. Such arrangements enable you get within one seat of any student, tend to make it easier for students to see visuals and one another, and are conducive to discussion. Many room arrangements are less than ideal and cannot be easily manipulated. In less than ideal rooms, work to keep students together in close proximity to you and any visual aids, and maximize your ability to move freely around the room. By utilizing the classroom space to its fullest, you move the focus of your student listeners and put more people in "front row seats" during the course of the session. Do not get trapped in the front of the room or in just one spot alone if you can possibly avoid it.

Agenda

Post a simple agenda for each class session. Students, like any listeners, occasionally fade out and lose focus on the conversation. An agenda will help them stay on track with your remarks and the progress of the session. The agenda can be used strategically to move students along, especially in cases where discussion flourishes, threatening to take over the class session in unproductive ways.

Eye Contact

Cultivate your ability to maintain direct eye contact with your students throughout each class session. Extemporaneous speaking demands direct eye contact between speakers and listeners—a skill essential to reading and responding to audience feedback during a speech performance. Direct eye contact also contributes to maintaining audience attention, and for instructors it serves as an effective classroom management skill. When students are behaving appropriately, your eye contact communicates your enthusiasm, energy, and personal engagement with students. When students are behaving poorly, a well-placed glare can produce favorable results in a student's ability to listen without disrupting the progress of the session.

Vocal Variety

Students worry that one characteristic in their voice will produce monotony—speed, pitch, volume, etc. They do not realize that vocal monotony occurs, not because a speaker speaks too quickly, too slowly, too softly, or too loudly, but because one speaks at one pace, one pitch, or one volume. To avoid instructional monotony, avoid long lectures. More important to modeling good presentational practice and classroom effectiveness, plan to use your voice strategically (not melodramatically) to enable students to listen better. Use pauses and welcome silence occasionally. Remember that *all* variations in speed, pitch, and volume can produce intended emphasis.

Classroom Audio-Visual Support

Speakers find audio-visual management one of the most important, yet difficult presentation skills to master. Many teachers struggle as well, or seem satisfied with mediocre employment of audio-visual support. Whether you are using chalk or computer-generated graphics, a cassette player or a sophisticated sound system, you should design, place, and manage your visual aids consistently according to the standards established in your textbook and applied in your evaluation forms for speeches.

Providing Speaking Models

From time immemorial, speaking teachers have used model speakers and speeches to help students grasp the art of public speaking. Reading manuscripts of excellent speeches can be of some value, but actually seeing and hearing examples of excellent public speaking is of greater value, especially for students who are acquiring extemporaneous speaking skills.

Famous Speeches & Speakers

Allyn & Bacon Classic and Contemporary Speeches DVD is an anthology of representative American speeches and speakers. It has more models than could possibly be used in the classroom in a term. The anthology is dominated by political speeches and covers the full range of public speeches identified by Aristotle—deliberative, forensic, and epideictic. The DVD can be used to teach exhortation, apologia, case-building, narrative, myth, and the use of figures and tropes. The format makes the anthology classroom-friendly and also allows easy repetition of speech segments used to show particular public speaking ideas and practices as they are enacted by real speakers. According to your own interests and time constraints, recording speeches related to current events in the term can also enrich the classroom. Public speeches are also available directly through Internet Web sites, through university and public libraries, and through bookstores (locally and online).

Student Speeches

Famous speakers and speeches provide helpful models and set high goals for public speaking students. These students also need to see how other students handle public speaking assignments like their own. The Allyn & Bacon *Student Speeches Video Library* provides a wide variety of student speeches and speakers presenting assignments much like the ones you are likely to assign. With permission, you may also want to show videos of student speeches from your school's public speaking courses during previous terms.

NOTE: *Select model speeches with care!* Many of the famous or student speeches may approach speaking situations in ways that will not be helpful to students in your class. For example, most famous political speeches are delivered from manuscripts, not extemporaneously. Also, instructors have different expectations for note management, visual aids, use of a podium, etc. Student speeches from other schools or even other sections of the course at your own school may model things you do not want your students to emulate.

Incorporating Technology

As levels of computer literacy and accessibility increase for students, instructors have more options for incorporating technology in the public speaking course. Technology options include presentation software that generates sophisticated visual aids, Internet research options, and speech design software.

Visual Aids

The technological standards for professional presentations have escalated dramatically as laptop computers and LCD projectors have dropped in price. Today, many workplace presentations include the expectation for computer-generated images to support presentations. How and to what degree will you incorporate these technologies into your course? Remember first that technology does not immediately make visual aids more effective; principles for

effective use of visual aids must be observed, regardless of the level of technological

sophistication. The default offerings on some software programs produce sophisticated color and

design options that are substandard for use in performance settings (small type, too many words

per slide, hard-to-read color schemes, excessive detail, etc.). Nevertheless, if students have good

access to visual technology, such visual options should be encouraged. Student proficiency with

computer software programs has escalated rapidly. Just a few years ago, instructors needed to

consider dedicating class time to introduce and teach basics about presentation software. Today,

if institutional resources are available to students and in the classroom, relatively sophisticated

computer-generated visuals can now be incorporated in public speaking courses with the

expectation that students can manage the software, enabling the instructor to concentrate once

again on the principles of visual design for public presentations.

Internet Research

The *Allyn & Bacon Quick Guide to the Internet for Speech Communication*, by Terrence

A. Doyle, and *iSearch for Speech Communication,* also available through Allyn & Bacon,

exemplify the kind of resources available to help students make the most of the Internet for their

public speaking courses. However, the volume of information does not guarantee the quality.

Consider how you can encourage students to extract sound, reliable, and worthwhile material

from the Internet information glut. Teach them to evaluate Internet sources according to the same

sorts of criteria they should be applying to conventional print sources they might find in the

library. You can lead students into wiser, more efficient use of the Internet in general—not just for your course—by taking some time to outline some basic tenets for Web use and holding students accountable to reasonable standards.

- What is the reputation of the publisher?

- Has the material been subjected to editorial review?

- Is the information available in print form?

Also, while Internet research grows in popularity, continue to expect students to utilize the many other good forms of speech research, including interviews, site visits, and traditional library research.

Components to Cultivate Student Interaction

Putting together a good class session combines a number of different factors: knowledge of the topic, good material to make the session meaningful, and the repertoire of instructional skills you possess to develop and execute a learning process that engages your students. If you have been appointed to teach this course, assume that you have access to basic knowledge and good material for the content of the session.

Therefore, the remaining aspect of excellent instruction would be how you manage the learning process in the classroom. Effective instructors weave content and process together in ways that appear effortless to students. But the actual weaving is far from effortless. A pivotal presupposition drives our concern with instructional processes: *People learn best when they interact with the material, the instructor, and other learners. Since public speaking, both conceptually and practically, demands consideration and application of human interaction, dynamic classroom interaction should be central to public speaking pedagogy.* Therefore, teaching public speaking well requires adoption of a closely related pedagogical objective: to create a classroom environment in which each student is invited to interact meaningfully with the instructor, classmates, and material.

Discussion

What kinds of things have instructors from your past done that stifled in-class discussion? A worst-case scenario might be one like the class in which a professor seemed to seek discussion, only to interrupt students in mid-sentence and berate them based on the teacher's inferences (often inaccurate) about what the remainder of the student's response would be. Straight lecture without opportunity for discussion would probably be better. But picking on poor practitioners is much simpler than developing good discussion management skills of our own. To make discussion work better as an instructional tool, use the suggestions that follow. However, none of the discussion ideas will work effectively until you yourself are convinced that discussion leads to better learning for your students. If you view discussion primarily as "shared ignorance" or a waste of time, then your discussions will never amount to more than being a charade or filler (and you will probably believe that the bright young minds in your class are dull, thoughtless, and unresponsive).

Open and Closed Questions

The most important single skill you can learn in discussion management is the difference between an "open" and a "closed" question. Closed questions prompt fixed answers, either a yes/no or a single correct answer. The responses, or lack of responses, are predictable. Students are not inclined to answer such questions out loud. For instance, consider the following dialogue as a typical closed-question discussion scenario. The instructor has made some introductory remarks about stage fright and wants to lead a discussion (statements in parentheses indicate unspoken responses in the minds of the students).

Professor: Do you fear giving a speech?

Students: (Yes.)

Professor: Can anyone tell us about a speaking experience you had and how you dealt with the nervousness?

Students: (No.)

Professor: Well, if you haven't given a speech yourself, are there ways that you have seen other speakers control their nervousness, or let their nerves take over?

Students: (Yes.)

Professor: It seems that you must have mastered the material from the book if you don't want to talk about it. You're awfully quiet this afternoon. Does anyone have any questions about stage fright?

Students: (No.)

Professor: What does the book say about why stage fright occurs?

Students: (I think it said something about a natural physiological response to a threatening situation, but I can't remember exactly—don't want to make a fool of myself today.)

Professor: OK. Let me list the strategies for managing stage fright on the board.

The professor in this class could go away thinking that the students were disinterested in the class session, unprepared, or just plain unresponsive. None of these assessments is necessarily accurate. As students in a classroom context, most people are unwilling to answer fixed alternative questions, even if they know the answer. In the scenario above, an extrovert might answer each of these questions, but by doing so he or she might well discourage everyone else from participating. This is particularly true of "Guess My Answer" questions. A Guess My Answer question is one in which the instructor has a single correct answer in mind. Experienced students have an intuitive sense for such questions and instinctively remain silent.

Closed questions are valuable to discussion management, but their primary purpose is to bring discussion to a close or make a transition to another topic. For example, if you want to close a discussion, say, "Does anyone have any other questions or comments?" If a person has an important point to make, he or she will speak. But in most cases, people will answer "no" in their own minds, say nothing, and allow you to move the session along. Closed questions

69

generally involve "to be" verbs (is, are, was, were, be, being, been), variations on "do" and "can," and any question that presents itself as a Guess My Answer variety.

Open questions invite people into discussion. They allow for many alternative answers. The very way one poses an open question should communicate the expectation for participation. An open question asks for opinions, ideas, examples, or any other sort of response that would enable a number of people to contribute personally. In a classroom setting, open questions should ordinarily be directly on task. For instance, an open question that could lead to significant interaction might go something like this:

Professor: What kinds of things do people fear might happen when they get up to speak?

Student A: They might forget what they were going to say.

Student B: Their voice might crack.

Student C: They might bore the audience.

Professor: OK. So we have a variety of reasons why people might fear public speaking. But why would any of these things be a problem in the real world—like in a speech that wasn't being graded?

Student D: Nobody wants to be embarrassed—there are all those people looking at you!

Student A: Yeah. And if it's a big speech at work, you might lose business or not get a promotion you wanted.

Professor: Any other ideas?

Students: (No.)

Professor: So there are personal and professional consequences we fear if we perform poorly

on a speech because of nervousness. Now, let's look at some specific

physiological responses associated with the perceived threat of public speaking.

(Lecture on physiological aspects of stage fright.) Now that we know that almost

everyone experiences stage fright to some degree, that apprehension is tied to our

physiological response, what sorts of suggestions have you heard or tried in the

past to deal with nervousness in public speaking situations?

In a process sense, these questions say, "Please let us know what you think." The

instructor should reinforce that message with tone of voice and other non-verbal indicators as

well. By doing so, the students understand that they can think out loud with their classmates

about the topic of discussion. They get actively engaged in the learning process without fear of

error or reprisal and can make a serious contribution instead. When you are ready to move the

discussion along, use a closed question and introduce the next issue.

As you attempt to use open questions to stimulate class discussions, write them out in

advance and test them on yourself. Can you come up with multiple good responses? If so,

include the questions in your lesson plan. If not, rework them until they meet your test. Initially,

always head into the classroom with at least your first few questions prepared. *Then recognize

that even well-prepared open questions will not prevent extroverts from dominating the

discussion unless you employ strategies to include input from the entire class.* The following

ideas will enable you to engage the entire class in the thought process and invite a wider variety of students to voice their input as a stimulus to their own learning and the learning of their classmates.

Writing-Before-Speaking

Picture a class of first graders. Anxious to answer questions in class, many have mastered the technique of raising their hands before the question is even complete, trusting that they will be able to come up with an answer on the spot. Some students never outgrow the practice and will try to answer every question you ask in class. However, many other students can make contributions if you create opportunities for them to gather their thoughts enough to offer a considered response.

Writing-before-speaking is one of the simplest and most effective ways to generate input from a cross-section of students or from each class member. It works on the assumption that almost everyone has something worthwhile to contribute, but that some people need a little more time to consider the issues for discussion—which means that their input is often bypassed. Here is how to use writing-before-speaking. First, let students know that you want them to write, then ask an open question to which you want them to respond. Allow ample time (a minute or so) for them to write a response. Watch until most of the students are done writing. Indicate that you are about to ask for responses. At this point you have a number of good options:

- Ask everyone to give their response (if it is a short answer type of question);

- Select randomly (e.g., everyone born in a certain month);

- Choose a few people who are ordinarily quiet, then open it up for discussion; etc.

By giving students time to write their thoughts, you guarantee that everyone has something to say, so speaking in class becomes less intimidating. It also allows you to include quieter members and to preclude domination of discussion by just a few people. I have also found this to be an excellent method for incorporating a variety of perspectives and maintaining balance in comments from men and women. The writing-before-speaking method need not compel you to hear from everyone on each question, but it does help students to stay engaged mentally and increase their readiness to participate. Once students are engaged in discussion, they also become more responsive and attentive to lecture segments in which the teacher develops ideas and takes students beyond their existing base of knowledge into new material. The principles behind writing-before-speaking allow for variations and use in combination with related methods to stimulate productive classroom discussion.

Partners and Small Groups

Instead of having students write, you can pose a question and have them discuss it first with a partner. Giving students time to discuss a pertinent question with one another gets each of them engaged, like writing, but also promotes interaction with one another. When you have a pair working together on a question or a problem, you are likely to spawn a number of perspectives and generate a different kind of feedback than when each student writes an individual response. You can poll groups for responses or return to a general discussion.

In some cases, you may decide to begin by asking students to write their own response to your question, but then have them discuss their responses within small groups. This method works particularly well with brainstorming activities—having each individual brainstorm for a minute or two, then create a composite list, and perhaps prioritize the group list before reporting or discussing with the class at large. Sometimes you may choose to limit the discussion primarily to the groups, and then continue with lecture or other activities.

Partner activities and small group discussion provide additional value in the learning process because students interact with the material and one another. Regardless of how many speak in a particular discussion that follows the partner or group activity, their minds are more likely to be stimulated and engaged as learners.

In-Class Speaking Exercises & Non-Graded Speeches

Public speaking students need performance training as well as conceptual depth. You can provide some of this training in non-graded experiences. Plan to incorporate some or all of the following sorts of exercises in your course: impromptu speaking, storytelling/example exercises, audience adaptation activities, how to cite sources in a speech, and introduction and conclusion exercises. In many of these cases, students can practice elements of their speeches that will eventually be performed for a grade. Most students will need to give impromptu speeches in the workplace, and many impromptu skills are transferable to extemporaneous speaking. The rest of the suggestions come directly from concepts and skills students routinely find difficult to execute. By practicing in class, you will help them to perform better and to know what and how to practice more effectively for speeches.

As noted in Chapter Two, provide informal feedback in the context of non-graded speaking exercises and assignments. Become accustomed to identifying excellent performances and noting gaps or inadequacies. *In both cases, use the instructional opportunity to teach why a performance would be evaluated as superior or explain how to improve on the deficiencies you identify.* While graded speech performances deserve personal attention, you can avoid favoritism and student embarrassment by making your comments after a group of performances and speaking in terms of patterns or themes you observed.

Group Activities

You will find a wide array of group activities in most public speaking textbooks. Allyn & Bacon includes such ideas in the Instructor's Annotated Editions and teacher's manuals that accompany their student textbooks. You may also find effective activities by talking to other public speaking teachers or you may develop your own activities. In any case, when you plan to use a group activity in class, make certain that you:

1.   Define the task clearly for students.

2.   Provide the steps necessary to complete the activity.

3.   Set a time limit.

4.   Establish a reporting mechanism.

Whether you do this on the board, via transparency or computer-generated image, or in a handout, following these steps will communicate your expectations for the exercise. Again, when you get students involved in a good group activity, you get them involved in the learning process and help them to better engage and process the material.

Micro-Lectures

Public speaking class must take students beyond merely awakening and reconfiguring what they already know. Therefore, lecturing plays an important role as a component in the classroom learning process. The exclusive lecture format has become a stereotype, perhaps because students perceive that such a format does little to stimulate a love of learning. But a well-placed and well-performed lecture can cultivate learning in students in ways that other methods cannot. Therefore, how instructors incorporate lecture material into a given class session makes a huge difference. First, get students engaged in the session through an introductory question, small group exercise, or other activity. Second, begin the lecture with what they already know and proceed into the new ideas or information the lecture is intended to provide. Third, limit any single lecture segment to ten minutes or so, after which students should have opportunity to work with the material in some way.

Homework Assignments

The quality of learning and participation in class can be greatly enhanced by careful use of assignments outside of class. For example, do you want your students to be prepared to discuss the reading for the day? Assign a few discussion questions from the end of the chapter to be collected in class. *Then use the questions for class discussion!* Other ideas include:

1. **Locate Examples:** Ask students to bring in examples for use in class, examples like good and bad evidence, good introductory material, means by which

76

messages can be adapted, good and bad visual aids, examples of appeals to logos, pathos, and ethos.

2. **Design Speeches Incrementally**: Incorporate steps of speech design and preparation into outside assignments. Make it impossible for students to procrastinate on the development of their speeches by requiring them to complete preparation steps as the steps are being taught. You can configure such assignments in a number of ways, to force students to apply instruction immediately.

3. **Debrief Their Speech**: Expect students to submit a review of their their own speeches as a lead-in to debriefing a speaking round with the class as a whole.

In all cases, keep your assignments closely tied to the material in the course, binding the conceptual material to the practice and performance aspects of public speaking.

Speaking Rounds

As noted earlier, speaking rounds constitute approximately one-half of the class sessions in most courses. Speaking days should be considered instructional days, i.e., lessons. Precious teaching time may be lost if you treat a speaking round as a speech contest, bypassing teaching opportunities in an effort to preserve "fairness" in evaluation. In my experience, grading does not vary in any noticeable way from the beginning to the end of a speaking round, despite in-round instruction. Specifics on speaking rounds will be developed in the next section. For now, keep in mind the value of demonstrating skills, raising questions for the class to consider, and responding to speakers in class with praise, evaluation, and direction. In other words, speaking rounds are prime teaching opportunities. Plan to use them that way.

Lesson Planning

When you are beginning as a teacher, you need to invest time and energy to move effectively through your first term. A lesson plan can help you to gain certainty about what each class session should accomplish and to gain confidence to implement the plan with skill. Furthermore, committing to a plan puts you in a better position to evaluate what works and what needs to be revised or replaced. Suggestions for how to build a simple, effective lesson plan follow.

Residual Message

What do your students most need to understand by the conclusion of the session? If they could only take one thing from class on that day, what should that one thing be? The one thing you identify is known as a *residual message*. Answer these questions and you will be on the road to a good lesson plan, because teaching public speaking should be more concerned with what students are actually learning than about an instructor somehow covering a certain body of material. At the top of your lesson plan, consider your answers to the questions above and write a complete statement that follows this form: At the end of today's class session, I want each of my students to understand that . . . Here is a sample residual message for a session on introductions, transitions, and conclusions: *At the end of today's class session, I want each of my students to understand that introductions, transitions, and conclusions are difficult for speakers to create and to execute well, but they are crucial components to enhance audience attention,*

understanding, and retention.

Specific Objectives

With the overall message in place, turn your attention to the two or three specific

instructional goals for the session. For example, teaching a session on introductions, transitions,

and conclusions might call for objectives concerning beginning and ending the speech

decisively, previewing and reviewing the body of the speech, and helping listeners to make

process and content connections between main points. Specific objectives should become your

main teaching points, necessary to communicate the residual message of the class session.

Session Agenda

How will the objectives be addressed in the actual class setting? At this stage you begin

to order the concepts and skills you will teach in the session. The session agenda must take into

account administrative details and other routine class activities like collecting papers or assigning

reading and other outside exercises. Establish a complete agenda for the session and frame it in

such a way that you could put the agenda on the board as a guide for students.

Working Agenda

The residual message, objectives, and agenda establish a master plan for the session. Now

you need to develop a script or game plan for instruction. With limited time and multiple options

to accomplish the day's objectives, you must turn your attention to making decisions about the specific use of lesson components. In other words, you must plan what to do within each agenda item to promote effective learning for students.

Item

Create a plan for each agenda item. The plan may involve only one activity or a combination of activities. Review the prior segment on lesson components to refresh your memory about a beginning set of options. Write out exactly what you plan to do, including discussion questions, group activities, or lecture notes. If you plan to write something on the board, write down what you want to put on the board and note that you intend to do so.

Time

Allot class time for each item and write down the allotment on the working agenda. Review the timing for the session as a whole. Allow sufficient time for start-up activity and explanations of assignments, agenda, etc. As you become more accustomed to teaching the course, you will become more accurate in your estimates. *Remember, speaking exercises, good discussions, and well-designed group exercises take a significant amount of class time.*

Rationale

Beneath each agenda item, write an instructional rationale for the specific component(s). Why did you choose to approach the item the way you did? How do you expect the particular activities in the item to achieve your goals for that agenda item?

Test for Success

Whenever possible, identify how you can assess the effectiveness of your approach to a particular item after the class is over. For instance, will you test on this material, will it appear in a speech preparation or evaluation assignment, or in the speech performances themselves? Not every activity or item will be easy to evaluate and some are impossible, so do not disqualify an instructional activity simply because you cannot figure out a way to evaluate it. At the same time, recognize that assessment of teaching effectiveness has been gaining importance both for individual instructors and for departments as greater scrutiny is applied to higher education nationwide.

First Day of Class

Paradoxically, the first day of class for a new instructor is crucial and entirely unimportant. As a new public speaking instructor, you can be rightfully concerned about how to negotiate the first day of class and start off on the right foot. On the other hand, no matter what you feel like, the instructional value of the entire term does not depend on how well you handle the first day. After all, many students on your first-day roster will not show up for class, and some may well add as late as 10 days into the term. But you will want to get off to a good start, so the following tips are provided to help you approach that first day of class with confidence.

Making the First Day Count

Plan to use the first class session in its entirety. First impressions are important, and making a good first impression is one of the reasons that new and seasoned instructors may both experience some anticipation on the first day of a new term. The first day provides an opportunity for you to set a positive tone and climate for the course immediately. You will want to build rapport with your students personally, but you should also take advantage of the day to create a favorable learning environment in other ways. Whatever and however you proceed, remember that you can provide instruction and get them involved in learning from the start.

Ideas and Options

Students should leave the first session with a clear idea of your expectations for their participation and performance in the course. They should also have a sense of the climate you are trying to establish and the basic coordinates they can use to navigate the term successfully. For example, if you want students to interact with you and one another throughout the term, make sure that you include those elements from the start. Are they going to be speaking in this class? If so, get them on their feet, even if only for fifteen seconds each. What do you want them to know about public speaking—both the course and the topic—before they leave your classroom on day one? Work it into the lesson plan. Do you anticipate boring them to tears each day? Pass out the syllabus and read it to them aloud in class.

Resist the temptation to have students introduce themselves. Self-introductions are one of the most difficult speaking assignments conceivable. Instead, have students introduce someone in class they have not met before (they get to know one another immediately), or have them talk about the worst or best speaker they have seen recently. Whatever the exercise, make it relevant to public speaking in some clear way. Introduce them well to what a class session in the course is like before they ever see a syllabus. A conventional way to handle the syllabus is to highlight key issues in it. Also consider dividing the class up into groups and assigning each group a page or section of the syllabus, asking them to decide what one thing is most important for their classmates to know from their assigned segment. Then open the class for questions about the syllabus and use the students' points and questions as leads for your comments on crucial issues in the course.

The first class also provides a natural opportunity for you to introduce your philosophy of teaching and explain why you are looking forward to the semester. If you have speaking experience, refer to it in the first class and remind students that you were not a one-day wonder as a speaker, even if you are quite polished today. If you have little public speaking experience yourself, neither apologies nor mentions of the fact are necessary. The course was entrusted to you for good reasons. Proceed on that basis to practice what you are teaching.

Planning

Prepare the first session using the same sort of lesson plan discussed previously. Plan to begin building the positive learning environment that you envision for the course. *If you propose to make the class an interactive climate, then get all of the students interacting within the first five minutes!* They will know that you expect them to participate and will be prepared to engage the ideas and skills in the course as long as you continue to lead them through the learning process. (If you start by reading the syllabus, say you want the class to be participatory, and then ask a closed question, at least acknowledge that you are sending mixed messages.)

Allow time on your first-day agenda for late arrivals and discussions with students about dropping and adding your course before and after class. Expect that not every student will have a book, even if they all should. Control the room arrangement as well. Orient the seating according to your plan for the term.

Because most public speaking classes are limited in size, you will be in a position to get to know your students by name. Beginning to learn their names on the first day will help you build rapport. Some teachers ask their students to complete index cards with personal information about major, hometown, career goals, and speaking experience. Others greet each student personally, hand out a syllabus, and write down the students' name as a means of taking roll on the first day. Whatever your strategy, establish a plan to start learning names and dealing with your students on a personal level.

Performing

Teaching is a performance. Instructors are not entertainers, but sound instruction includes elements of performance which contribute to the sense of anticipation you will feel as the first day of class approaches. Enjoy the performance. Recognize that you are participating in an ancient educational ritual, teaching a course in which you can help your students gain a competency that will stay with them throughout their lives. Public speaking *is* critical to maintaining the democratic freedoms cherished by Americans. The first day of class provides you with an opportunity to invite students into a new, sometimes fearful, but rewarding venture. Your performance will set the pace for them, and in the first performance you begin to enact for them what you have planned for the course to become for them as individuals and as a class.

Chapter Four:
Evaluation and Grading

Public speaking courses customarily include speech performances, written examinations, and an assortment of other assignments. This chapter prepares instructors to consider their approach to speaking rounds, to evaluate and grade speech performances, and to design examinations for the public speaking course.

Speaking Rounds

The instructional value of a speaking round has been mentioned, but not developed. The performance aspect of the course demands that we consider the related pedagogical issues, namely, the speaking rounds. Do not confuse teaching about how to design a speech with instruction about speech performance. You can teach much about performance through activities and exercises. But speaking rounds provide extensive opportunities for performance instruction, and students are likely to be attentive when so much is at stake for them personally. To focus on grading alone may be easier—to remove the coach/teacher hat and wear only the judge hat. But if you focus only on grading, you will have abdicated many wonderful instructional opportunities. Of course, by using both hats in a speaking round you accept some tricky dynamics. But if we profess to be more concerned with learning than with grading, we must accept this set of difficulties.

Speech Days as Teaching Opportunities

The teaching opportunities come when students are thinking about the most important parts of public speaking while they listen to their classmates and perform their own speeches. Part of your job is to keep them involved in the process each day of the speaking round. Be prepared to raise germane questions and to entertain the questions of your students. The inquiry may occur in the open classroom, through your evaluations or peer evaluations, or from student reviews of their own performances (using videotape). However, students are not likely to view speaking rounds as learning opportunities unless you prompt them to do so by your words and actions. Build up speaking days as the highlight of the course and push your students to stay engaged in the process throughout, especially when they are not assigned to speak.

Variations on Speaking Round Formats

Choose speaking round formats that fit best with your instructional objectives. People vary the structure of speaking rounds depending on what they are trying to accomplish. For example, some teachers provide all the instruction necessary to complete a series of four speeches, finishing all reading, non-speaking round class sessions, and testing in the first half of the term. Students present their speeches for the remainder of the term. Another approach brings students together in a large lecture format for instruction on public speaking theory and speech design. Students are divided into lab sections in which to present their speeches. Most instructors integrate speaking rounds between conventional instructional sessions throughout the term. Using this model, instruction on informative speaking precedes an informative speech round, and then instruction on persuasive speaking is followed by a persuasive speech round, and so on.

Interspersing instruction and performance, with a speaking round dedicated to the type of speech allows a range of options for structuring a round. The first choice to make is how to handle the sequence of speeches. Some teachers allow students assigned to a given day to speak consecutively, and then provide commentary for all at the end of the class session. This method assures that time will permit all speakers to complete their speeches with plenty of time to spare for comments each day in class. The instructor can be selective about comments and can address certain global issues evident in more than one of the speeches. Student comments, if included in the process, can be somewhat depersonalized.

A second approach, the one I recommend most highly, sets aside a certain amount of time for each speaker, including performance and feedback time. For example, a five-minute speech would take about ten minutes of class time with commentary. Therefore, a class of 24 students would require six speaking days. Using this approach, speakers present their speeches and receive immediate feedback before the next student proceeds. Each student receives individual attention from teacher and classmates, and the performance can be used as an instructional tool for the entire group, keeping a focus on the issues at hand concerning public speaking. When something particularly good happens, the instructor can commend it. When a common difficulty emerges in a performance the teacher can consider it with the class constructively.

Taking speeches one at a time with commentary allows for a number of options during the comment period. In every case, assume that the instructor will take the lead on oral feedback. The options include:

1. Will students complete written evaluations? (All students or a selected group may write peer evaluations.)

2. Will students provide oral feedback? Will student feedback include constructive criticism or be limited to positive elements of the presentation?

3. Will speakers respond to Q & A? (A good idea in at least some rounds, since Q & A sessions are the rule in most public presentations and because human discourse expects a response.)

Each speaking round may be different, and probably should be, since the instructional objectives for each speaking round should be different. The time constraints must be carefully observed to make sure that all the speeches planned for the day can be presented. Choose some means of keeping students who are not speaking involved, whether writing comments, providing oral feedback, or raising questions.

Preparing Teacher and Students

Students should never be surprised by what transpires in the speaking round process. Establish a routine for your speaking rounds and explain the plan clearly to students, including what you expect from students who are not speaking on a given class day.

Note on Models: As discussed in Chapter Three, students should be somewhat familiar with your grading expectations from your response to speaking exercises and commentary on model speeches. *Consider setting aside time before graded speeches begin, to show a model speech in its entirety. Follow with an explanation of how the evaluation and grading process works.* Use a speech from the *Classic and Contemporary Speeches* DVD or the *Student Speeches Video Library* available through Allyn & Bacon.

If you have not already done so in a course packet or handout, make sure that students have a copy of the evaluation form you will use to evaluate their speeches and the general criteria for grading speeches. *(A sample handout on general grading criteria appears at the end of Chapter Three.)*

Speech Evaluations

Public speaking instructors must develop a unique pedagogical skill: grading speeches. Speech evaluations require more than assigning a grade. But learning how to assess a speech, assign a grade, and *justify the grade* to yourself and your students constitutes one of the greatest challenges for new instructors. This segment breaks down the process of evaluation into more manageable parts. *(See the sample evaluation form at the end of this chapter and note how the form corresponds to the major elements of speech evaluation that follow.)*

Summative and Formative Evaluation

First, understand that a good speech evaluation includes both a summative evaluation, a grade, and formative evaluation—comments to help the student improve their next performance. The summative evaluation is your judgment. You coach through formative evaluation. Most of the concerns that speech instructors harbor regarding evaluation evaporate when both types of evaluation are practiced with care.

How to Assign a Grade

New instructors fear grading because speech grades seem more vulnerable to the charge of subjectivity. However, when evaluation is approached with care, grades can be justified according to the form and substance of the performance. The classroom evaluation environment is ordinarily much more forgiving than the workplace. Furthermore, students should be gently reminded that the course prepares them for life outside of the classroom, in which audiences respond to speeches more subjectively, but still make evaluations that routinely change the course of personal lives and occasionally change the course of history.

Clarify your standards; teach students how to meet your standards, and grade according to criteria that match your standards. The most effective way to ease student concerns about the speech grading process is to evaluate students according to criteria for generally discernable elements of the speech process *that you teach them to perform in preparation for the speech*. For example, if you expect them to include a preview of their main points in the introduction to their speech, teach them what a preview is and explain the range of acceptable performance behaviors. ("You don't need to say, *my first main point is… my second main point is… my third main point is,* but you must somehow make your main points clear enough that a careful listener could write them down.") Then include the presence and quality of a preview in the evaluation criteria. The same goes for visual aids, supporting material, audience adaptation, structure, reasoning, etc.

Students worry most about delivery. They worry that teachers will downgrade them heavily because they cannot win the class fashion contest, or have a voice problem, or have trouble making eye contact. Like everything else, delivery should be included in the criteria, but once students realize that you can tell whether they organized their speeches well and use good sources—even if their knees are knocking the whole time—most will relax about grading. In reality, most of the things we want them to do can be done well, even with some delivery snafus. Eventually, they will understand that the smooth talker with poor organization and little substance could get a *D*, while someone who prepared and presented an outstanding message but lacked gestures and was still working against vocal monotony could get into the *A* range.

In addition to formulating specific criteria, provide a global sense of what students need to do to achieve a certain grade. For example, if a student includes every required element, but without any distinction or creativity, that should place him or her in the *C* range. A speech oozing with creativity and energy, but lacking in a few areas, might be a *B*, and so on. (The first page of the sample evaluation form is dedicated to summary evaluation; the second page is dedicated to formative evaluation.)

Whatever sort of evaluation form you use, document what did and did not happen in the speech according to your criteria. Then aim for strict consistency in how you apply the standards. Soon, you will develop a feel for the grade range in which a speech belongs (summative evaluation) and have full confidence in explaining both how the student earned the grade *and how she or he might improve the next performance to get to a higher level* (formative evaluation).

Writing Comments

The quality and tone of your written comments concerning the speech probably play a role as important in student perceptions of grading fairness as defining and documenting evaluation standards. Make sure to include space on your evaluation form for *formative* comments. In fact, all your written comments other than your notes taken during the speech should be coaching comments, things that worked well in the performance and suggestions for improvement on the next one.

Note as many areas of success and identifiable potential as you can. Each can be mentioned briefly. But feel no compulsion to mention every problem you observe. You neither have time, nor can you stimulate much positive progress by doing so. When addressing problems, stick to two or three issues. As in many skill-training situations, correcting one major problem may solve many others. For instance, poorly managed note cards often cause poor eye contact, reduce the speaker's animation of expression and gesture, and result in vocal monotony. Dealing with the note management problem may strengthen the performance in a number of ways. Time management problems point to underdeveloped research, poor structure, lack of focus and discrimination in message development, or poor practice habits. Think about the root cause, limit your comments to that problem, and minimize or omit commentary on the time issue (even though the student may have lost points to speaking too briefly or too long).

Regardless of the grade, you should make suggestions that demonstrate genuine concern for helping the student to improve as a speaker. Even *A* speeches allow you to take students to new levels of performance, urging them to explore new territory in delivery or to attempt different speech structures or strategies. In this way, your students will come to appreciate your knowledge of public speaking and personal attention. Therefore, you may well soften the reality of a low grade by providing multiple insights that prove you do not cast them in one grade range without any hope for a higher grade.

Responding as a Listener

In addition to evaluative comments, include a personal response to the message in every written evaluation. Demonstrate that you were being attentive to more than the criteria, and respect the student as a speaker in his or her own right. A speech may spark a memory, a thought, or a question. You may share an experience about yourself that the student could not have known. In persuasive speeches, you may agree, disagree, raise related issues for yourself, etc. This is also the place where you can register your listening enjoyment and appreciation. You elevate the significance of the speaking event and humanize your classroom by doing so.

Grading and Videotape

Nothing builds credibility for your speech evaluation skill like videotaping student speeches. If possible, videotape every speech. Have students supply their own tapes and do not review the tape yourself. Record the speeches for students' benefit. Videotaping provides a wonderful opportunity for students to grow through self-evaluation. In my experience, videotape also radically alters student perceptions of the quality of speech evaluations from their teachers. The predominant comment instructors get from students goes something like this, "When I saw your evaluation of me, I didn't think that I had done the things you said; then I watched it and I couldn't believe it. Everything you wrote was true and I thought you were actually too easy on me." Although this rarely happens, if a student ever claimed that a teacher had missed an element in a speech, they could review the tape together and clarify the situation.

Testing

Will you include tests in your course? If so, why and how? Most public speaking textbook instructor's manuals provide test questions. Some provide test bank software. The question of how to incorporate testing into your course cannot be solved by these resources. The reasons why you test will help you determine the type, frequency, and development of your quizzes, tests, or exams.

Objectives

Tests can play a number of different instructional roles. We most commonly think of tests as a means of assessing conceptual understanding in students. But tests can also be used as a learning tool and as a simple means to prompt students to keep up with their reading. You may use exams for any or all of these purposes in public speaking. However you incorporate testing into your course, identify your objective and keep it in mind during test design.

Types

Multiple choice, true-false, short-answer, and essay questions are conventional and serviceable types of items for traditional in-class examinations to assess conceptual understanding. Obviously, a test can be constructed of all one sort of test item or of some combination. Your choices will affect the length of time students need to complete the test and the kinds of assessment the test will provide.

Because of limited class time and the nature of the material, take-home exams are well suited to the public speaking course. For instance, exams in which students are asked to make choices that help them understand speech design process or how to build a good argument can be done at home, open-book, and advance the learning process beyond what the constraints of class time allow.

Testing for reading comprehension also places a premium on learning outside of class. Students habitually neglect textbook reading. Tests to push them into the text motivate them to explore the benefits offered in texts—like the many examples, applications, and fine points on public speaking—that cannot and should not be covered during class time. *Once students discover that they will be accountable for the reading assignments, they read, and do so much more carefully.*

Frequency

If you are testing for conceptual understanding, test at natural unit breaks during the term. From this standpoint, a midterm and a final would be sufficient, although you may choose to give an additional exam or two. If you are using a take-home test as a learning tool, it should correspond with the specific topic or process you want students to learn. Take-home tests require more grading time, so use them sparingly unless you have the extra time. Reading comprehension tests or quizzes should be simple to give, take, and grade. They should be more frequent, because students should be urged to keep up with the reading. Allowing too much time between such tests tempts students to fall behind on their reading.

Development

With your objective in mind, construct your exam to accomplish your purposes. Remember these basic tenets:

1. *Value the test and the items within the test equitably.* Consider using five point values whenever possible. Five or more points per item will result in clearer distinctions between scores when you grade the test and will prevent complaints over "just one point."

2. *Remember the time constraints within which your students must complete the test.* Whether you test in class or give a take-home test, avoid frustrating students by giving them too much test for the time allotted.

3. *Assume that if you give them a test that is an easy mark, students will be tempted to cheat.* Create two versions of the test with identical questions, but put the questions on different pages. Such adjustments are simple in the age of word processing.

4. *Whatever you construct must be graded.* Be careful to assign only the essay questions to which you are willing to devote much time. Also, to ease and speed the grading process, ask short-answer questions with definitive answer components.

SAMPLE SPEECH EVALUATION FORM

Date:		Speaker:			
Elapsed Time:	:	Topic:			
		Comments	**—**	**√**	**+**
ORGANIZATION Does the speech include the necessary elements (introduction, transitions, and conclusion)? Is the structure of the speech evident, well-balanced, and does it develop the residual message?			☐	☐	☐
SUPPORTING MATERIAL Does the speech contain appropriate reinforcement for the points through which the residual message is developed? Does it include a variety of evidence from sources cited by the speaker?			☐	☐	☐
AUDIENCE ADAPTATION Is the message adjusted specifically to the needs and interests of these listeners? Are adjustments and connections to listeners made in each segment?			☐	☐	☐
PHYSICAL BEHAVIORS (Delivery) Does the speaker support the verbal message with non-verbals that enhance and do not detract from it?			☐	☐	☐
VOCAL VARIETY/ARTICULATION Does the speaker use rate, pitch, and intensity to maintain interest? Are the words clear and is the grammar proper?			☐	☐	☐
VISUAL AIDS Is the speech supported by legible, simple, clear visuals? Are the visuals managed without distracting from the message?			☐	☐	☐

THINGS THAT WORKED WELL . . .

SUGGESTIONS FOR NEXT TIME . . .

COMMENTS. . .

Speech Grade_____

NUMERICAL EQUIVALENTS				➜	➜	➜	**Numerical Equivalent** _____
A+	100	C	75				**Overtime/Undertime (-10)** _____
A	95	C-	71				
A-	91	D+	68				**Unapproved Topic (-15)** _____
B+	88	D	65				
B	85	D-	61				**Missed Due Date (-25)** _____
B-	81	F	50				
C+	78						**TOTAL PROJECT SCORE** _____

Note: This evaluation form has been adapted from NCA standards for the competent speaker, Moreale et al., 1993.

Chapter Five:
Dealing with Challenges

How do you expect your public speaking teaching to affect your attitudes and performance in other responsibilities? Where do you expect to find healthy integration? Where do you expect to experience tension? In this chapter, we will consider how best to navigate the course as one responsibility among many in the instructor's life. For example, some new instructors focus narrowly on the content of the course and the teaching performance within each class meeting, neglecting other pedagogical matters which are just as important as in-class instruction. Such everyday teaching challenges frequently arise for new instructors. Some are unavoidable, while other problems teachers invite upon themselves. By preventing or anticipating their emergence, you can negotiate these challenges and turn many into opportunities.

Teaching with Limited Speaking Experience

If you have been appointed to teach public speaking, a lack of personal experience in public speaking would naturally make your entry into the classroom more challenging. If you find yourself in this situation, remember that you are teaching the course because the department believes you are qualified. Your best qualification may be your ability to learn the material quickly and completely enough to stay two steps ahead of the class. In your first few terms, you can teach students how to learn by learning with them. Still, you are probably more concerned about performance than conceptual material. First, your classroom itself serves as a routine opportunity for you to develop speaking experience. Include a well-prepared lecture segment (5-

15 minutes) as part of each class session and treat it as a formal presentation. The students need not have any indication of what you are doing, but you can build confidence quickly, both as a speaker and an instructor by practicing *as* you preach. Second, look for opportunities to speak outside of the classroom context. Whether you join a Toastmasters' Club or seek out and accept speaking engagements, try to get more "real world" experience giving speeches.

Integrating Teaching and Scholarship

If you are a graduate student with a teaching appointment, tension between your roles and responsibilities as teacher and scholar are inevitable. Both roles require good performance to maintain your status and these roles continue as long as you remain in the profession. You must find ways to *teach your strengths*. By doing so, you will prepare your lessons with greater efficiency and pleasure.

First, concerning your areas of interest in the field, do not alter the syllabus radically, but do teach the material from perspectives most familiar to you. For example, if you are studying organizational communication, bring that emphasis to the public speaking context. If you are studying political communication, by all means introduce speeches and other kinds of political presentations as examples. If you study small group communication, incorporate a group project and presentation. If you study argumentation, pay particular attention to teaching strong argument skills through the course. Obviously, the syllabus must still include the basics of public speaking, but bring the best of your knowledge into the classroom where it fits, and see if you can do so without getting caught!

Second, concerning your scholarship, consider how you can incorporate good, pertinent literature appropriate for generally educated audiences. Such sources can include original works on rhetorical and communication theory as well as novels, historical documents, philosophy, etc. By doing so, you can add conceptual depth and common textual material to the course from which to draw examples, generate discussion, and stimulate good speech topics.

If on any given day you see your teaching responsibilities as a necessary evil, take a mental health day and relax a bit. If you develop a persistent attitude toward teaching as merely a vehicle to keep you in school, or as a take-it-or-leave-it enterprise, do yourself and your students a favor and get out of the field entirely.

Time Management

Teaching has long been considered a profession. As a professional, you are accountable for your own time, which brings a wealth of potential for freedom, flexibility, and frustration. Looking at how you manage your time can often tell you how well you are managing your teaching, especially in reference to your other responsibilities. If you are an adjunct, your duties may already be well defined and your time available for the public speaking course may be set. However, many new instructors must balance a full load of graduate courses and teach two sections of public speaking. The following time management suggestions apply to both adjuncts and graduate students, but are particularly important for teachers with more discretion in their schedules:

1. **Always return speech evaluations at the next scheduled class session.** To destroy credibility and student rapport, be chronically late in returning speech evaluations. To maintain the respect of your students and your own sanity, commit yourself to grading speeches from each session before the next session.

For the same reasons, *commit to a return date for other graded assignments* (not necessarily the next class session).

2. **Allow 15 minutes per speech on written evaluations.** Work to get under 10 minutes per speech. Students need you to identify their problem areas and point them toward how to improve. They need a brief response to the content of their speeches. What you can write in the first ten minutes is probably what will help them to improve most.

3. **Block out a routine time in your schedule for lesson planning and grading.** Make the block large enough for heavy days. Better to have time left over than to neglect instructional duties or other responsibilities.

4. **Use office hours for public speaking administrative work.** Update your grade book, review simple assignments, make arrangements for audio/visual equipment, set up a speaking order; whatever administration the course requires, plan to use office hours to accomplish the mindless tasks. Some days a number of students will visit, but other days you will have the whole time to yourself. Do course-related work that permits interruption.

5. **Never procrastinate on other work by devoting unplanned time to public speaking.** People who enjoy teaching and struggle with coursework or research can be prone to spend more time than they should on the course and neglect their other duties. For many instructors, teaching provides immediate gratification, especially when students respond and grow through the term. Coursework and research require greater perseverance, and produce fruit at a slower pace.

Therefore, people who know better may still spend too much time on teaching, to their own detriment. Keep your public speaking time in perspective.

Student Problems

During the upcoming term:

- one student will profess intense fear of public speaking;

- another student will become clinically depressed;

- many will experience the death of grandparents;

- a number will claim that they will lose a scholarship if a grade is not elevated;

- some will miss weeks of class with mononucleosis; and

- a few will become course design critics.

Ordinarily, no section of the public speaking course will have more than two or three of such cases, but it is hard to predict which ones will surface. Here are a few tips on how to deal with each of these commonplace student problems:

1. **Apprehension:** When students fear that they will not be able to perform at all because of speaking apprehension, take them seriously. If the following conditions are true in your course (and they should be) reinforce them with an apprehensive student: a) everyone experiences some apprehension as they learn to speak in public; b) most people fear delivery aspects of the course; c) delivery is not nearly the most important criteria for grading, especially in the early speeches; d) the type of public speaking they will be learning (extemporaneous)

will help them not to have to worry about forgetting their main ideas or losing their place in the speech; e) you can help them as they work through the speech design process and practice their speeches before presenting them in class.

Occasionally, students experience such severe apprehension that they may need to be assigned to a special section of the course, if available at your institution. However, with encouragement and help, most students can succeed in the course, especially if you demonstrate creativity and flexibility in dealing with such cases.

2. **Mental Health Issues:** Because public speaking classes tend to be smaller than many, especially at large universities, students may come to you with personal difficulties. You must discern whether these are relatively routine matters or larger issues. For instance, romance problems are one thing, but if a student begins to talk about involvement in an abusive relationship, help is needed beyond what most instructors are trained to provide. Know the numbers for the counseling professionals at your institution and do not hesitate to refer students. In fact, be prepared to be a resource to provide the link students may need to get help.

3. **Personal/Family Matters:** If a student claims that a grandparent has died, believe it. Never ask for an obituary. Traditional college students are at a stage of life in which grandparents die and other family issues routinely emerge. In one semester, I had three freshmen students, the youngest in their families, each of whom had parents divorce the month after college started. Instructors are better off allowing themselves to be conned in such situations than to challenge wrongly a single

grieving student. Offer help to such students by urging them to report their situation to academic advisors or whoever notifies teachers officially concerning excused absences for such reasons, and extend as much flexibility as possible to help these students to complete their coursework.

4. **Grades:** Certain students need to maintain a set grade point average (GPA) to meet a variety of goals. You should proceed with your grading oblivious to these individual matters. At the end of the semester, a student or two may arrive in your office saying, "If I don't get a ___ in this class, I will not be . . ." They may ask for special opportunities for extra credit to raise the grade. Students may question an earlier grade (and if you have instituted a sensible grade complaint policy, you will have an easy answer and rationale). A few brazen souls may request special consideration and make a case for raising the grade simply because of their situation. Remember that the grade in public speaking is rarely, if ever, the only grade in question. Unless you make a calculation error in the course grade, the responsibility for the mark lies squarely with the student. Do not fall for the pathetic appeal.

5. **Illness:** Again, traditional students operate in patterns and living situations that seem to make them more susceptible to illness. Instructors should attempt genuine flexibility and generosity in such cases, but primarily with students who deal responsibly with participation and attendance by promptly informing you when they must be absent and by working hard to make up missed work. You can appropriately ask for some sort of documentation from people who give evidence of abusing the excuse. Producing a note from a doctor or a health center is not

nearly as traumatic as being asked to produce an obituary to prove a loved one's death.

6. **Course Complaints:** Every so often a student may come to your office and explain to you how the course should be taught. These students may actually believe they are the last hope for saving you from yourself. They may have a problem with your classroom manner, the textbook, the number of speeches, other assignments, or any number of other aspects of the course. Check your impulse to correct such students quickly. Listen carefully. You may gain unexpected insights into how students experience the course. In most cases, a student's distress is real and the course is a part of the stress. That does not mean that you should necessarily adopt any of the suggestions. But by listening first and refusing to take offense at the many offensive things such students are capable of interjecting, you may gain insight into yourself as an instructor and the course. Plus, you may help the student to perform better and learn more, even if conditions do not change dramatically.

Instructor Pitfalls

What difficulties can you avoid? The potential pitfalls are many, and few are exclusive to inexperienced instructors. But the routine pitfalls surround student rapport, classroom management, and teaching tangents.

Student Rapport

Most people want to be liked. As new instructors, many of us are tempted to make a priority of being liked by our students. We want our students to trust us and enjoy our class, a pretty natural response when trying on a new role for size. Instructors without much distance from their own undergraduate days feel the tension between acceptance and authority most keenly. Of course, students should not despise their instructor—that is not the point. But work to win student approval *as their instructor*. Follow this rule: If all of your students like you all of the time, you are probably not challenging them enough.

You can select from a variety of strategies to focus your relationship with students on your student-teacher interaction. Consider symbolic issues like your wardrobe, how students can contact you, how you prefer to be addressed, and your language. You may feel uncomfortable initially having students call you *Ms.* or *Mr.* On the other hand, you may feel less comfortable at the end of the term when a student comes in and challenges a grade on a first name basis. But whatever you decide about these issues, do not make the error of socializing with your students during the semester in other-than-official contexts. Develop your social relationships with graduate students if you are a graduate student and with other faculty members if you are an adjunct professor. Also develop social relationships with people off campus.

Speech Grading

As we have seen, grading includes extra dynamics and intensity in public speaking because of the performance component of the course. Therefore, instructors face a number of pitfalls associated with neglect or violation of basic grading principles discussed in previous chapters.

Late Return of Graded Speeches

Commit yourself to return speech grades at the class meeting following a student's speech. Students invest much emotional energy when they prepare a speech. Typically, they pay close attention to the time it takes for you to return their speech evaluations. They deserve a predictable turnaround time on their performance evaluations. Fair or not, in my experience students employ prompt return of their speech evaluations as a litmus test concerning the competence of their instructor. In particular, instructors who lack diligence in this one area of grading seem to experience the swiftest, most serious loss of respect from students.

Critique without Formative Comments

Focus your written comments on what students can do to improve their performances, rather than merely listing mistakes. When you assess a speech, no pretense is necessary. You can address the problems head-on. But do so with an eye to provide instructional comments that help the student see the solution as well as the problem.

Favoritism

Apply your standards consistently across the board. Some students quickly sense that they will not get a fair evaluation because they belong to the wrong campus organizations, are involved in the wrong activities, or in some other way have fallen out of the good graces of an instructor. Despite the fact that students' concerns about such favoritism are unfounded in most cases, experience shows that public speaking instructors must conscientiously work against favoritism in every form, especially because students put so much of themselves on the line personally in public speaking.

Unclear Expectations

Take time to prepare students for speech grading by introducing your grading criteria, form, and process in advance. If you begin grading speeches without familiarizing students with your expectations, you may be deluged with questions about speech grades, if not outright complaints. Use the grading process as a teaching opportunity, exploiting student interest in grades to highlight ideas that they may have missed previously.

Grade Inflation

Initially place speeches into broad *A, B, C, D, F* categories and use the *C* range as your default grade. Because most workplace speeches on any given day are mediocre, do not grade by subtracting from an assumed *A*. Begin with a *C* and only move the grade to a higher range if the speech positively merits elevation. Forget about plus and minus grades until you have placed the speech in a broader category. Many inexperienced instructors contribute to grade inflation by evaluating an *A* speech as an *A+*, a *B* speech as an *A*, and a *C* speech as an *A-*. This approach does not mean that you will not end up with many *A*s and *B*s. But most workplace speakers have never had a college-level public speaking course.

Too Much Time Grading

Allow yourself a fixed amount of time to grade speeches and stick to it; limit yourself to 10-15 minutes per speech to grade and write comments. Work to gain discipline in the speech grading process to give students the best insights you can offer. Remember that students can only process and respond usefully to a limited number of comments—too much detail can derail improvement. Resist the temptation to procrastinate on other work by putting too much time into grading speeches.

Student Misdemeanors

When students behave inappropriately in class, how will you handle it? Avoid embarrassing students, even if they may have earned the embarrassment. Instead, use the return of a written assignment to send a message concerning minor problems. A brief, direct e-mail message may also have a favorable effect. During class, move to a quick group activity and divide problem pairs or sets of students by placing them in different work groups. If student conflict flares up (e.g., verbal conflict) avoid taking sides and emphasize process control and rules for civil dialogue. In other words, avoid direct personal confrontation as much as possible. If necessary, arrange a meeting after class.

Course Process Comments

Avoid making process comments about your own attitude toward the course, especially if you are operating within a structured syllabus designed by the course director. You need not like the design. But voice your personal concerns about the course structure or policies to the director or department chair. You in no way benefit your students by voicing your concerns to them.

Using Public Speaking as a Front

Occasionally, instructors would prefer to be teaching another communication course—perhaps a theory course, criticism course, or some other area of specialty. Whether you work from a departmental syllabus or develop your own, teach public speaking. You may gain greater satisfaction by teaching your favorite material, but your students will not be well served. Yes, teach your strengths, but teaching your strengths does not equal using the public speaking course as a front for the course you most aspire to teach.

Ideological Pulpiteering

Will you seek to help your students to find their public voices, or do you expect them to parrot *your* public voice? At a recent conference, a series of speakers advocated the use of a similar introductory course in a closely related field to proselytize students to a particular ideological position. The panel suggested that readings, assignments, and class discussions be used as a means for "consciousness-raising" among impressionable students. Challenge your students with new perspectives that might provoke new ideas and cultivate critical thinking. But resist the temptation to use the course for your personal political purposes.

Free Speech Issues

How do you deal with a student who wants to advocate a position that you find problematic? First, you are responsible for the classroom, and the classroom should stimulate learning and approximate real-world circumstances simultaneously. Respect the mission of the institution regarding your classroom policies on speech topics. Second, you may rightly insist that your students not promote violation of the law in your classroom and prescribe other constraints on props and visual aids (for instance, no firearms or facsimiles thereof).

Religious speeches often pose vexing problems for public speaking instructors. Regardless of your personal religious convictions (or lack thereof), religious speeches need not raise such concerns, and the freedom of speech for a student committed to a religious topic need not be violated. Simply structure your assignments to make a simplistic religious speech that would seek to proselytize a captive audience a poor selection. Then welcome a religious topic that satisfies the assignment. Most religious students will accurately read a prohibition against all religious speech as a violation of the First Amendment. But if you guide a student from a weak approach to the assignment to a stronger way to address the assignment with a religious topic of their choosing, they may well respond with a presentation satisfactory to both student and instructor.

Chapter Six:
Support Resources

As a public speaking instructor, one of the most practical issues you face is lesson planning—preparing solid sessions for your students. Each of the Allyn & Bacon public speaking textbooks listed below is available in an instructor's annotated edition (IAE) or is accompanied by an instructor's manual. Both IAEs and instructor's manuals supply ideas for exercises, activities, and test items.

Earlier in this manual, I noted the importance of teaching your strengths and, as a new instructor in the public speaking course, you may benefit greatly by looking at how other A&B textbooks, training manuals, and support materials present the same topics covered in your primary textbook. A brief description of Allyn & Bacon's public speaking textbooks below is followed by a matrix showing the correlation between chapters in A&B texts available for your use as you prepare each lesson.

Allyn & Bacon Public Speaking Texts

Public Speaking: An Audience-Centered Approach

Steven A. Beebe, Southwest Texas State University
Susan J. Beebe, Southwest Texas State University

This text's audience-centered approach is the major theme that guides the speaker through the speechmaking process by emphasizing the importance of analyzing and considering the audience at every point along the way. Numerous examples, excerpts, and sample speeches support the instruction. Featured narratives by professionals, "Speakers at Work," exemplify ways to adapt and succeed in challenging scenarios. Information on adapting to diverse audiences, a chapter on ethics, and technology for research and visual aid preparation equip students to manage public speaking throughout their professional lives.

The Essential Elements of Public Speaking

Joseph A. DeVito, Hunter College of the City University of New York

Distinctive in its emphasis on cultural issues and critical thinking, this text maintains close connections to the real world of public speaking. DeVito incorporates advice from experienced public speakers plus the latest technological advances in research, planning, and audio-visual support. The text emphasizes listening skills and ethical issues as they relate to public speaking. One of the most thorough texts available, DeVito helps students achieve early success in the basic course and then cultivates depth of knowledge and skill as the term progresses.

Principles of Public Speaking

Kathleen German, Miami University of Ohio
Bruce E. Gronbeck, The University of Iowa
Douglas Ehninger
Alan H. Monroe

Founded on principles of public speaking established by Alan Monroe and Douglas Ehninger, this text emphasizes critical listening skills and audience analysis in diverse cultural contexts from which good speeches can be designed. Kathleen German and Bruce Gronbeck incorporate the most contemporary issues in public speaking, from the matters of ethics and diversity to Internet research, to complement this textbook's enduring pertinence to the needs of students in the basic course.

Mastering Public Speaking

George L. Grice, Radford University
John F. Skinner, San Antonio College

This text uses an engaging style to guide students through the speechmaking process. The authors emphasize critiquing speech through the analysis of public speaking examples, excerpts, and sample speeches. The "Speaker's Journal," consisting of a series of interviews with a student speaker at various points in the speechmaking process, examines his self-critiquing process. Another theme, the ethical contract between speaker and audience, is provided through a separate chapter on ethics and "Ethical Decisions" boxes, aimed at stimulating classroom debates on the difficult choices facing public speakers and listeners.

Principles and Types of Public Speaking

Raymie E. McKerrow, Ohio University
Bruce E. Gronbeck, The University of Iowa
Douglas Ehninger
Alan H. Monroe

Students encounter public speaking with attention to conceptual depth and culture studies through the most recent edition of a textbook that has been a standard for the basic course for more than 50 years. In their update of the book, the authors incorporate contemporary theories and concerns with ethics as they impact public communication. This textbook integrates established principles with cutting edge electronic research methods and presentation technology to ground students in the art of public speaking while preparing them for today's speaking contexts.

Public Speaking: Strategies for Success

David Zarefsky, Northwestern University

Zarefsky encourages students to think through and about their strategies in the public speaking process from a conceptual framework grounded in rhetorical theory and criticism. Students are urged to consider the diversity of audiences, occasions, and speakers, and to choose a specific purpose, a relevant topic, and the appropriate material to make their speeches successful. "Applying Strategies" boxes illustrate how students can apply the strategies approach to speaking. "Choose a Strategy" boxes build upon concepts and skills introduced by asking students to apply a strategy to various speaking situations.

Allyn & Bacon Public Speaking Textbook Topic Matrix

Topic	Beebe & Beebe	DeVito	German	Grice & Skinner	McKerrow	Zarefsky	PowerPoint* Transparencies
Introduction to Public Speaking	1 App A	1	1,2	1	1	1	T1, T4-7
Ethics and Public Speaking	3	Integrated	Integrated	2	Integrated	1	
Diversity and Public Speaking	1		1,4	5	3, 4	3	
Speech Design Process	2	1	2	3	2	1	T11-12, T19-20
Speaking Apprehension	2	1	1,2,10,12	3	1	1	T2-3
Listening	4	2	3	4	3	2	T8-10
Audience Analysis	5	5	5	5	5	3	T13-18
Topic Selection	6 App B	3	2	6	2	4	T21-25
Researching the Topic	7	Integrated	6	7	6	5	T26-27
Using the Internet	7	3,5,6,7	6 Integrated	7	6	5 Integrated	
Supporting the Message	8	4	6	8	6	6	T28-31
Organizing the Body of the Speech	9	6	7	9	7	7	T32-33
Intros, Conclusions, and Transitions	10	6	8	10	8	8	T37-43
Outlining	11	6	7	11	9	9	T34-36
Language	12	7	9	12	10	10	T54-57
Delivery	13	8	10	13	12	11	T44-53
Visual Aids	14	4	11	14	11	12	T80-100
Informative Speaking	15	9	12	15	13	13	T58-59
Persuasive Speaking	16	10	13	16	14	14	T60-67
Reasoning	17	Integrated	14	17	15	6	T68-74
Ceremonies and Special Occasions	18	11	15	18	16	15 App A	T75-76
Small Group Speeches	19	12	15	19	16	15	T77-79
Speech Criticism and Analysis	3	2	3	4	3	2	
Sample Speech Texts	App C	Integrated	Integrated	App	Integrated	App B	

* This column refers to the *Allyn & Bacon Public Speaking Transparency Package*—100 full-color transparencies to provide visual support for classroom lectures and discussion. PowerPoint electronic support is also available at www.ablongman.com/suppscentral, including the *PowerPoint Presentation Package*, a set of text-specific lecture outlines by Dan Cavanaugh, and the *Allyn & Bacon PowerPoint Presentation Package for Public Speaking*, a package of 125 slides and user guide.

Allyn & Bacon Public Speaking Support Materials

Allyn & Bacon provides a wealth of supporting materials tailored to the specific A&B public speaking text you or your department has adopted. To locate the supporting materials dedicated to your A&B text, look for the *At-A-Glance* grid located in the Instructor's Manual. Also visit the Allyn & Bacon Web site at www.ablongman.com to review the extensive support materials available for public speaking instructors and students.

NOTES

NOTES

NOTES

NOTES